W9-ACC-812

WEST BEND LIBRARY

1st EDITION

Perspectives on Modern World History

The Tiananmen Square Protests of 1989

1st EDITION

Perspectives on Modern World History

The Tiananmen Square Protests of 1989

Jeff Hay

Editor

GREENHAVEN PRESS
A part of Gale, Cengage Learning

GALE
CENGAGE Learning™

Detroit • New York • San Francisco • New Haven, Conn • Waterville, Maine • London

WEST BEND LIBRARY

Christine Nasso, *Publisher*
Elizabeth Des Chenes, *Managing Editor*

© 2010 Thomson Gale, a part of Gale, Cengage Learning.

Gale and Greenhaven Press are registered trademarks used herein under license.

For more information, contact:
Greenhaven Press
27500 Drake Rd.
Farmington Hills, MI 48331-3535
Or you can visit our Internet site at gale.cengage.com

ALL RIGHTS RESERVED.
No part of this work covered by the copyright herein may be reproduced, transmitted, stored, or used in any form or by any means graphic, electronic, or mechanical, including but not limited to photocopying, recording, scanning, digitizing, taping, Web distribution, information networks, or information storage and retrieval systems, except as permitted under Section 107 or 108 of the 1976 United States Copyright Act, without the prior written permission of the publisher.

For product information and technology assistance, contact us at
Gale Customer Support, 1-800-877-4253.

For permission to use material from this text or product, submit all requests online at
www.cengage.com/permissions.

Further permissions questions can be e-mailed to permissionrequest@cengage.com

Articles in Greenhaven Press anthologies are often edited for length to meet page requirements. In addition, original titles of these works are changed to clearly present the main thesis and to explicitly indicate the author's opinion. Every effort is made to ensure that Greenhaven Press accurately reflects the original intent of the authors. Every effort has been made to trace the owners of copyrighted material.

Cover images © Peter Turnley/Corbis. Reproduced by permission.

LIBRARY OF CONGRESS CATALOGING-IN-PUBLICATION DATA

The Tiananmen Square protests of 1989 / Jeff Hay, book editor.
    p. cm. -- (Perspectives on modern world history)
  Includes bibliographical references and index.
ISBN 978-0-7377-4796-6 (hardcover)
1. China--History--Tiananmen Square Incident, 1989--Juvenile literature. I. Hay, Jeff.
  DS779.32.T558 2010
  951.05'8--dc22
                                       2009041850

Printed in the United States of America
2 3 4 5 6 7 14 13 12 11 10

CONTENTS

YA
951.058
T43h

CHAPTER 1

Historical Background to the Tiananmen Square Protests

Tiananmen Square began to wane in late May 1989, leaders revived enthusiasm by bringing into the square a sculpture resembling the Statue of Liberty.

Tiananmen Square crackdown was an important moment in contemporary China's attempt to meld a restrictive, one-party political system with a mostly free-market economy.

CHAPTER **2**

Controversies Surrounding the Tiananmen Square Protests

standing of China's brand of communism. Although their intentions were admirable, their demands for democracy were "premature." The article's authors do not mention the violent end to the demonstrations.

The last governor of the British colony of Hong Kong, which was returned to China in 1997, claims that China's economic development will ultimately require its authoritarian government to "adjust." To support this view, he cites a Chinese leader who was ousted from power for encouraging leniency over the Tiananmen Square demonstrators.

The Nobel Prize–winning economist argues in 2002 that China, in contrast to ostensibly democratic Russia, experienced great economic growth in the 1990s by speeding up a transition to free-market practices. He notes that this has not led, however, to greater political freedom.

The controversial publication of the Tiananmen Papers in 2001 showed the world the ways in which China's leaders decided to respond decisively and harshly to the pro-democracy demonstrations of spring 1989. Many questioned, however, the origin of the documents upon which the Tiananmen Papers were based.

FOREWORD

"History cannot give us a program for the future, but it can give us a fuller understanding of ourselves, and of our common humanity, so that we can better face the future."
— *Robert Penn Warren,*
American poet and novelist

The history of each nation is punctuated by momentous events that represent turning points for that nation, with an impact felt far beyond its borders. These events—displaying the full range of human capabilities, from violence, greed, and ignorance to heroism, courage, and strength—are nearly always complicated and multifaceted. Any student of history faces the challenge of grasping the many strands that constitute such world-changing events as wars, social movements, and environmental disasters. But understanding these significant historic events can be enhanced by exposure to a variety of perspectives, whether of people involved intimately or of ones observing from a distance of miles or years. Understanding can also be increased by learning about the controversies surrounding such events and exploring hot-button issues from multiple angles. Finally, true understanding of important historic events involves knowledge of the events' human impact—of the ways such events affected people in their everyday lives—all over the world.

Perspectives on Modern World History examines global historic events from the twentieth-century onward by presenting analysis and observation from numerous vantage points. Each volume offers high school, early college level, and general interest readers a thematically arranged anthology of previously published materials that address a major historical event, with an emphasis on international coverage. Each volume opens with background information on the event, then presents the controversies surrounding that event, and concludes with first-person narratives from people who lived through the event or were affected by it. By providing primary sources from the time of the event, as well as relevant commentary surrounding the event, this series can be used to inform debate, help develop critical thinking skills, increase global awareness, and enhance an understanding of international perspectives on history.

Material in each volume is selected from a diverse range of sources, including journals, magazines, newspapers, nonfiction books, personal narratives, speeches, congressional testimony, government documents, pamphlets, organization newsletters, and position papers. Articles taken from these sources are carefully edited and introduced to provide context and background. Each volume of Perspectives on Modern World History includes an array of views on events of global significance. Much of the material comes from international sources and from U.S. sources that provide extensive international coverage.

Each volume in the Perspectives on Modern World History series also includes:

- A full-color **world map**, offering context and geographic perspective.
- An annotated **table of contents** that provides a brief summary of each essay in the volume.
- An **introduction** specific to the volume topic.
- For each viewpoint, a brief **introduction** that has notes about the author and source of the viewpoint, and that provides a summary of its main points.
- Full-color **charts**, **graphs**, **maps**, and other visual representations.

- Informational **sidebars** that explore the lives of key individuals, give background on historical events, or explain scientific or technical concepts.
- A **glossary** that defines key terms, as needed.
- A **chronology** of important dates preceding, during, and immediately following the event.
- A **bibliography** of additional books, periodicals, and Web sites for further research.
- A comprehensive **subject index** that offers access to people, places, and events cited in the text.

Perspectives on Modern World History is designed for a broad spectrum of readers who want to learn more about not only history but also current events, political science, government, international relations, and sociology—students doing research for class assignments or debates, teachers and faculty seeking to supplement course materials, and others wanting to improve their understanding of history. Each volume of Perspectives on Modern World History is designed to illuminate a complicated event, to spark debate, and to show the human perspective behind the world's most significant happenings of recent decades.

INTRODUCTION

On June 5, 1989, the world's attention was riveted by photographs and film footage of an incident that had just taken place on Chang'an Avenue in Beijing, China. There, on that wide street outside the city's Tiananmen Square, a single, unarmed man was photographed standing in front of a line of the heavy tanks of China's People's Liberation Army. Apparently, this one man had, by himself, stopped the movement of the tanks, sent into action by a Chinese government seeking to take control of a city divided by protests. The pictures of this "Tank Man" remain among the most vivid images of the pro-democracy protests in Communist China in 1989, and the man himself was later deemed by *Time* magazine to be one of the 100 most influential people of the twentieth century.

In that one year, 1989, the governing system known as communism was dealt a near-mortal blow. That year, Communist governments across Eastern Europe, which had ruled since the post–World War II years of the late 1940s, collapsed one by one, with the fall of the Berlin Wall the greatest symbol of those events. Even the Soviet Union, the first major Communist power and a nation whose military might had propped up communism in Eastern Europe since World War II, had calls for reform in 1989. Communist leaders there also witnessed the first stirrings of the disintegration of the Soviet empire, a process that was complete by 1991.

The People's Republic of China, the world's second-largest Communist power, was also rattled by calls for the sorts of democratic reforms arising elsewhere in 1989. But these calls, made mostly by university students during April, May, and June of that year in Beijing's

Tiananmen Square, were violently silenced by China's government. The students' protests, which had been reinforced by tens of thousands of ordinary citizens, ended with a crackdown involving China's People's Liberation Army. The toll of those who died or were wounded in the crackdown, and the number of those arrested afterward, is still unknown. Unlike the Soviet Union or its Eastern European satellite states, China remained a one-party Communist dictatorship.

Communism, described most thoroughly and famously by Karl Marx in the nineteenth century, promised to create states where all citizens were economically and socially equal. But the twentieth century leaders who tried to implement Marx's ideology generally ended up creating intolerant dictatorships instead.

In China the Communist insurrection was led by Mao Zedong, who modified Marx's ideology by claiming that the Communist revolution could be carried out by rural peasants, if properly led, rather than urban industrial workers. Mao's revolutionaries built up masses of support in China's countryside, where most people lived and worked, and their efforts resulted in a Communist takeover of China in 1949. Mao's new regime was, and continues to be, known as the People's Republic of China.

Even though Mao's revolution was at heart a peasant one, he realized that China needed to be an industrialized nation for true communism to emerge there. From the 1950s on, China has, with some setbacks, industrialized rapidly, using at first the top-down methods common in dictatorships. In these, governments try to guide and control the process of economic development. From 1958 to 1961 Mao's government enacted a so-called Great Leap Forward designed to speed up this transition. The Great Leap Forward emphasized the building of heavy industry and infrastructure, and it also transformed the countryside through the creation of thousands of rural commientes. But bad planning and misallocations of basic resources, even food, resulted in the deaths of millions from starvation and disease.

Another misguided program, the Cultural Revolution of 1966 to 1976, brought still more strife to China. The Cultural Revolution was designed by Mao to reemphasize Communist thinking in a population that, to his mind, appeared to be losing the revolutionary fervor of 1949. It was targeted at younger people, many of whom joined groups of active revolutionaries known as Red Guards. The Red Guards, in turn, were used to try to upset China's social norms and traditions. Many long-standing monuments were destroyed or defaced. Students were urged to seize control of their classrooms and inform on older people, even parents, who seemed to lack revolutionary zeal. Those of the educated classes, meanwhile, were often sent to the countryside to engage in farm labor at the still-existing communes. The Cultural Revolution wound down by 1976 with few results and, in the estimation of many Chinese leaders who followed, it was a lost decade, especially in terms of economic development.

China's Communist leadership embarked on a drastically new course in the years following Mao Zedong's death in 1976. Mao's eventual successor as the head of the Communist Party of China was Deng Xiaoping, the leading politician in the nation from 1978 to 1992, and the true head of the Chinese government during the Tiananmen Square crackdown in 1989. Under Deng, China slowly abandoned strict state control of the economy, giving way to ever-increasing free-market activity. These reforms have resulted in China having the world's fastest growing economy over the last thirty years. As of 2009, China has the world's third-largest economy, after the United States and Japan, and is the world's top manufacturer of many industrial and consumer products. China's population, meanwhile, has grown increasingly urbanized and prosperous.

This economic development has not been accompanied by political reforms. Deng and his successors have emphasized what they consider a "socialist market" system, which combines free enterprise in economic activity with one-party control of government. For the leaders of the People's Republic, this represents a truly Chinese form of socialism, one in which a strong state maintains firm order and stability while releasing the energies of individuals to build new businesses and, when possible, even enrich themselves. In such a system, advocates argue, the Western version of liberal democracy is neither applicable nor appropriate.

Before 1989, modern China had gone through other periods when there were wide calls for Western-style reforms. Long before the Communist takeover, back in 1919, large numbers of university students staged what was to be called the May Fourth Movement, advocating strong nationalism and greater social equality. In the 1950s, China's new Communist leadership opened the country to diverse ideas on social, cultural, and economic issues in the Hundred Flowers Movement. Leaders believed that China would flourish if they encouraged a "hundred flowers to bloom," meaning a wide variety of viewpoints to be put forward and tested. While the May Fourth Movement enjoyed modest success and created small traditions of national unity and student protest, the Hundred Flowers Movement was deemed a failure. Mao disapproved of the criticisms of his government that appeared and engaged in a crackdown targeting thousands of people.

Students began a new wave of activism in the 1980s, demanding greater political openness to accompany the economic freedom then promising to enrich China. Many of them believed that, of necessity, political and economic freedom went hand in hand, as this had been the experience of Western nations since the late 1700s. Their first large-scale demonstrations took place in 1986 and 1987. Students complained about government's strict controls of even small aspects of their daily lives, voiced concerns about corruption at high levels, and argued that the People's Republic's elaborate bureaucracy stood in the way of democratic reforms. A top official who was sympathetic to calls for reform, Hu Yaobang, was forced to step down from his post as general secretary of the Communist Party of China and, in effect, to take the blame for these protests.

Hu Yaobang died on April 15, 1989, and state officials planned for a funeral in his honor for April 22. University students in China's capital of Beijing, whose hopes for reform had received encouragement in recent months by the writings of such dissident leaders as Fang Lizhi and Wang Dan as well as the stirrings of reform in Communist Eastern Europe, almost spontaneously began to use Hu's death as the occasion for new demonstrations. The first took place on April 15, when a small group of students gathered at the Monument to the People's Heroes in Tiananmen Square. By April 22, some 100,000 students had joined the protests and similar movements had arisen in other Chinese cities.

The Tiananmen Square protests lasted for seven weeks and received widespread attention around the world. Although the protesters had little in the way of a specific program of reforms to advocate, their youth and apparent willingness to sacrifice garnered a great deal of sympathy. Indeed, at two key points protest leaders like Chai Ling and Wu'er Kaixi took memorable steps to try to maintain the momentum of the demonstrations. One, beginning on May 13, was a hunger strike eventually involving up to one thousand people. Another, on May 30, was the unveiling in Tiananmen Square of a 33-foot-tall statue greatly resembling the Statue of Liberty. Made by Beijing art students, the protesters called the statue a "Goddess of Democracy." Meanwhile, Chinese leadership, mostly composed of men in their 60s, 70s, and 80s, proved mostly unwilling to negotiate with the protesters, with the one exception being Zhao Ziyang, general secretary of the Communist Party of China.

On May 20, Deng Xiaoping had declared martial law and sent units of the People's Liberation Army into Beijing to maintain control. Dissent within the Communist Party's ruling politburo, or policy-making committee, delayed direct action on the army's part, but eventually Zhao Ziyang was ousted and the decision made to use military force to disperse the protesters. The emptying of Tiananmen Square began late in the evening of June 3 and lasted until the dawn hours of June 4. Some students were killed or wounded, but most of them, after tense negotiations, agreed to leave the square.

The greatest number of victims of the crackdown were apparently nonstudents, ordinary Chinese people who engaged in their own protests, angry at their government for being so ready to use overwhelming force against students. Among them may well have been the "Tank Man" of June 5. His specific identity, as well as his ultimate fate, remains unknown. He may still live freely, or he may have been one of the hundreds, if not thousands, of Chinese people killed or imprisoned in the aftermath of the Tiananmen Square protests.

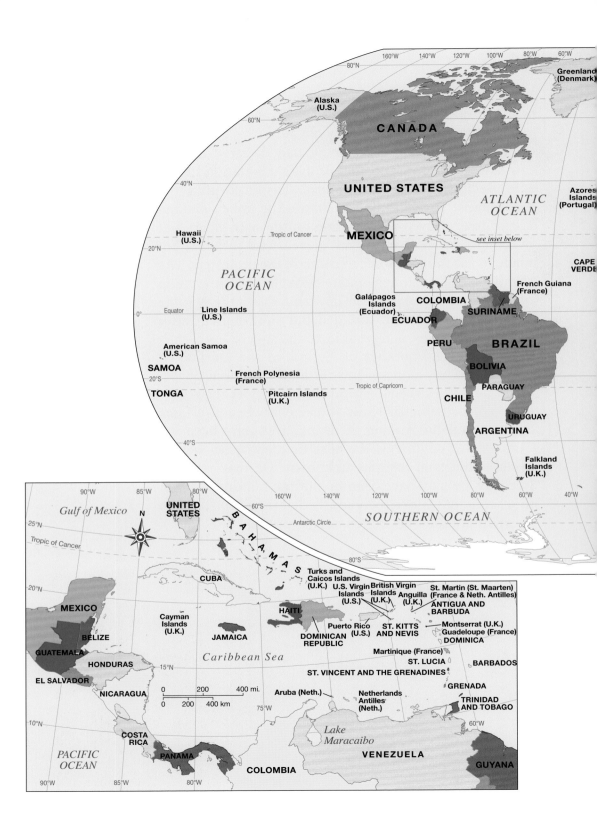

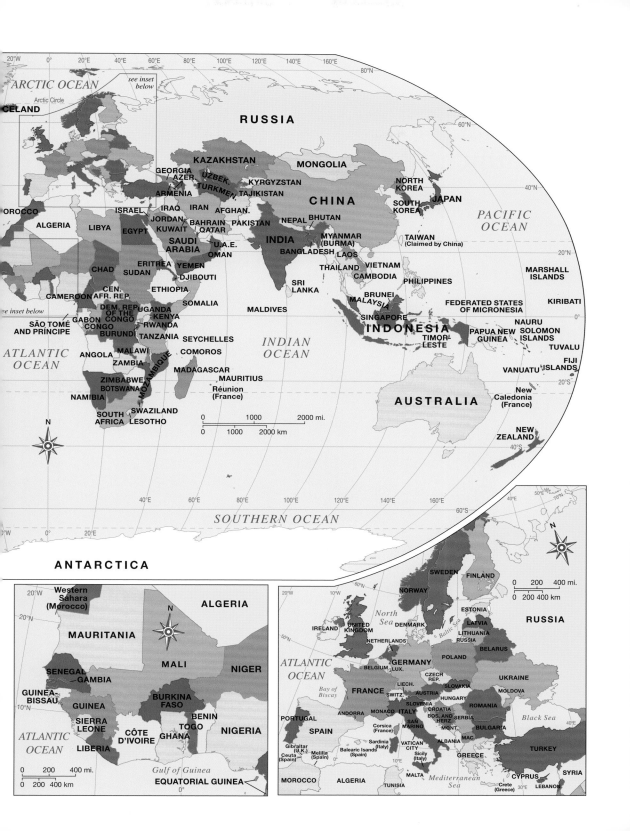

CHAPTER 1

Historical Background to the Tiananmen Square Protests

Peaceful Protest in Tiananmen Square Grows and Leads to Violent Oppression

Itai Sneh

By 1989, young people in China, most notably university students, were ready for political reforms. Although their nation had undergone economic changes that were then in the process of loosening up the Communist system's many restrictions, China remained a one-party dictatorship controlled by a small elite. As the following selection reports, students in China's capital of Beijing gathered in the city's vast Tiananmen Square on April 15, 1989, following the death of a reforming politician. What followed were weeks of growing protests and, finally, a violent government crackdown. As scholar Itai Sneh indicates, these events received wide attention from the outside world, but the U.S. president at the time, George H.W. Bush, preferred to

Photo on previous page: On Beijing's Tiananmen Square, student leader Wang Dan holds a news conference as he and his fellow dissidents occupy the plaza. (**AP Images.**)

SOURCE. Itai Sneh, *Dictionary of American History*. New York: Charles Scribner's Sons, 2003. Edited by Stanley I. Kutler. Copyright © 2003 Charles Scribner's Sons. Reproduced by permission of the author.

focus his attention on China's economic growth, as did Bush's successor, Bill Clinton. Itai Sneh is an assistant professor of history at the City University of New York.

> The scope of the largely non-violent opposition to the government was very broad.

On 15 April 1989, students held a vigil in Beijing's Tiananmen Square that commemorated the death of Hu Yaobang, a progressive leader who had sought reforms in China. They demanded freedom and empowerment for a young generation. The vigil became an ongoing protest in the square on 4 May and gave rise to a prodemocracy movement throughout China. Calling for a change in government through political liberalization and an end to official corruption, the demonstrators displayed Lady Liberty, meant to resemble the Statue of Liberty in New York Harbor and signaling a desire for an open way of life. Although the situation was far from a civil war, the scope of the largely nonviolent opposition to the government was very broad.

While the movement earned support for its agenda and sympathy abroad through wide international media coverage, the most potent challenge to the legitimacy and authority of the Communist Party since Mao Tse-tung's 1949 victory against the Nationalists was crushed at Tiananmen Square by military force on 3 and 4 June 1989, seven weeks after it had begun. Hundreds of protesters and bystanders were presumed dead, thousands wounded and imprisoned. From documents smuggled out of China and published in the United States, it appears that factional struggles among China's leaders and the fear of international shame delayed military action. President George H.W. Bush, acting upon public outrage, imposed minor diplomatic sanctions, but he subordinated human rights concerns to U.S. business

interests, encouraging Bill Clinton to denounce him as "coddling dictators" during the 1992 presidential campaign. In turn, however, Clinton's policies followed the pattern of engaging the Chinese commercially, claiming that trade and openness would facilitate political reforms. This policy was embodied in the ongoing grant of most-favored-nation trade status to China, the jailing of human rights activists notwithstanding.

A desire to honor deceased political reformer Hu Yaobang, whose portrait students placed on the martyrs' monument at Tiananmen Square, drew many early protesters to the site in spring 1989. (**AP Images.**)

Student Demonstrations Began Several Years Before the Tiananmen Square Incident

Paul Theroux

In the mid-1980s, novelist and travel writer Paul Theroux spent about a year traveling through China. He used trains almost exclusively, which allowed him to speak to hundreds of ordinary people and to see everyday life in China in ways most tourists never do. Having traveled through parts of China in 1980, when the oppressive legacies of Mao Zedong and the Cultural Revolution of 1966 to 1976 were still clear, Theroux found a very changed China by 1986. He sometimes spoke to university students, who by 1986 were already demonstrating in favor of democratic reforms.

In the following selection, Theroux reports on a return visit to Beijing, then called Peking, following a look at the Great Wall

SOURCE. Paul Theroux, *Riding the Iron Rooster: By Train Through China*. Washington, DC: G.P. Putnam & Sons, 1988. Copyright © 1988 by Paul Theroux. Reprinted by permission of The Wylie Agency LLC.

of China in the country's north. Visiting Beijing University, he found that students were playful and curious but at the same time maintained grievances against the Chinese government. One student predicted that more demonstrations were coming. Paul Theroux is the author of many novels, including *The Mosquito Coast*, *Blinding Light*, and the novella collection *The Elephanta Suite*. His travel books include *The Great Railway Bazaar*, *The Happy Isles of Oceania*, and *Ghost Train to the Eastern Star*.

Because it is a flat, dry, northern city, at the edge of Mongolia, Peking [Beijing] has beautiful skies. They are bluest in the freezing air of winter. China's old euphemism for itself was *Tianxia*, "All Beneath the Sky"—and, on a good day, what a sky! It was limpid, like an ocean of air, but seamless and unwrinkled, without a single wavelet of cloud; endless uncluttered fathoms of it that grew icier through the day and then, at the end of the winter afternoon, turned to dust.

Thinking it would be empty, I went to see the Great Wall again. Doctor Johnson told Boswell [two eighteenth-century English commentators] how eager he was to go to China and see the Wall. Boswell was not so sure himself. How could he justify going to China when he had children at home to take care of?

"Sir," Doctor Johnson said, "by doing so [going to China] you would do what would be of importance in raising your children to eminence. There would be a lustre reflected upon them from your spirit and curiosity. They would be at all times regarded as the children of a man who had gone to view the Wall of China. I am serious, sir."

The Wall is an intimidating thing, less a fortification than a visual statement, announcing imperiously: I am the Son of Heaven and this is the proof that I can encircle the earth. It somewhat resembles, in intention, the sort of achievement of that barmy man who gift wrapped the

Golden Gate Bridge [an artist named Christo]. The Wall goes steeply up and down mountainsides. To what purpose? Certainly not to repel invaders, who could never cling to those cliffs. Wasn't it another example of the Chinese love of taking possession of the land and whipping it into shape?

> 'There will be more [demonstrations]. . . . Many more.'

Anyway, the Wall was not empty. It swarmed with tourists. They scampered on it and darkened it like fleas on a dead snake.

That gave me an idea. "Snake" was very close, but what it actually looked like was a dragon. The dragon is the favorite Chinese creature ("just after man in the hierarchy of living beings"), and until fairly recently—eighty or a hundred years ago—the Chinese believed dragons existed. Many people reported seeing them alive, and of course fossilized dragon skeletons had been unearthed. The dragon was a good omen and, especially, a guardian. It is one of China's friendliest and most enduring symbols. The marauding dragon and the dragonslayer are unknown in China. And I found a bewitching similarity between the Chinese dragon and the Great Wall of China—the way it flexed and slithered up and down the Mongolian mountains; the way its crenellations looked like the fins on a dragon's back, and its bricks like scales; the way it looked serpentine and protective, undulating endlessly from one end of the world to the other.

From the Great Wall to Beijing's Student Protests

On the way back from the Wall I decided to stop at Peking University, where there had been student disruption. The campus was at the edge of the city, in a parklike setting, with pines and little man-made hills and a lovely lake. The lake was frozen. Skinny, panting students, with red cheeks and bobbing earflaps, slipped and skated on the ice.

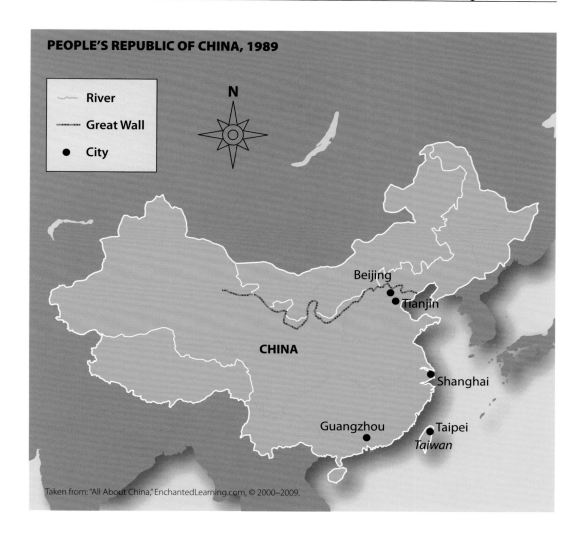

PEOPLE'S REPUBLIC OF CHINA, 1989

~~~ River

----- Great Wall

● City

N

CHINA

Beijing

Tianjin

Shanghai

Guangzhou

Taipei

Taiwan

Taken from: "All About China," EnchantedLearning.com, © 2000–2009.

I watched them with an American teacher named Roy who said, "They *do* have grievances. They want to believe what they read in the papers and hear on the news. At the moment, they get it all from the [foreign broadcasters] VOA [Voice of America] and BBC [British Broadcasting Corporation]. They want to trust their own government—and they don't. They want to believe that the reforms that have begun with Deng [Xiaoping, China's leader] are going to continue."

There were three theories to explain the sudden student discontent. One: that, as Roy said, the students really did have grievances. Two: that the government was divided and the students were being used by the liberal elements to test the conservatives. Three: that the disruptions were the work of conservative elements who wanted to discredit the liberals.

I was persuaded that the students had demonstrated on their own initiative. Their grievances were genuine but muddled.

"They were really frightened," Roy said. "They didn't think they'd be arrested, but some were. They didn't think the police would push them around—but the police beat some of them and abused others. They know that if it happens again they will be arrested and not released. That scares them. It means they'll be kicked out of the university."

"The right to demonstrate is written into the constitution," I said.

"Sure, but it requires five days' notice, and the students have to submit their names in advance," Roy said. "So the government will know exactly who the ringleaders are."

The students were going around and around on the ice, shrieking and skidding.

"There won't be any more demonstrations," Roy said. "They're too scared. But it was interesting. They tested their freedoms and discovered they didn't have any."

Cautious Students

The students would not tell me their names—well, who could blame them for being suspicious? They stood on the ice of Weiming Hu and became circumspect when I changed the subject from the weather to their discontent.

One boy told me he was "a small leader." He said he was a philosophy student and had been in the demon-

Photo on next page: Although the student protests at Tiananmen Square are modern China's best known ones, the democracy movement got its start by 1986 in places such as Shanghai. (AP Images.)

stration as well as its aftermath, when about 500 students had returned to Tiananmen Square and held a vigil from the night of January first until the early morning of January second, when the news came of their fellow students' release from police custody.

"Our teachers support us but they are afraid to say so," he said. "Officially they are said to condemn us. But the government misreports everything. They said there were three hundred students in the first demonstration when there were actually three thousand."

I said, "Do you think this repression is an effect of socialist policies?"

"I am not allowed to answer that," he said. "But I can tell you that the trouble with a lot of Chinese students is that they don't have a will to power."

Perhaps he was quoting Nietzsche from his readings in philosophy. And then I asked whether he thought that the students were too frightened, as Roy had said, to hold any more demonstrations.

"There will be more," he said. "Many more."

A moment later he was gone, and I talked with other students. They were jolly, frozen-faced youngsters on old, floppy skates. To ingratiate myself with them I borrowed a pair of skates, and seeing me fall down and make an ass of myself, they became very friendly. What did I think of China? they asked. How did American students compare with Chinese students? Did I like the food? Could I use chopsticks? What was my favorite city in China? They were goofy and lovable, with crooked teeth and cold, white hands. When I asked them whether they had girlfriends they averted their faces and giggled. They did not seem like counterrevolutionaries.

Students Bring a "Goddess of Democracy" to Tiananmen Square

Nicholas D. Kristof

In May 1989, Chinese university students and their supporters occupied Tiananmen Square in vast numbers demanding democratic reforms. Inevitably, some protesters were more enthusiastic and committed than others, and by the end of the month the numbers in the square began to wane. After first considering ending the occupation of the square in response to both the lessening intensity of the protests and to the poor living conditions there, student leaders decided to remain until June 20, the date of an important government meeting. The great symbol of this renewed protest was a model of the Statue of Liberty made by art students and dubbed by the protesters the "Goddess of Democracy and Freedom."

In the following selection, originally published on May 30, 1989, New York Times reporter Nicholas D. Kristof describes

SOURCE. Nicholas D. Kristof, "Chinese Students, in About-face, Will Continue Occupying Square," *The New York Times*, May 30, 1989. Copyright © 1989 by The New York Times Company. Reproduced by permission.

the atmosphere of Tiananmen Square in the late days of the protests, with a focus on the statue of the goddess. Kristof notes that such a symbol resonated with many people in a culture filled with protective spirits. He also notes that the protesters enjoyed clear support from some of Beijing's inhabitants.

> A crowd of nearly 100,000 workers and students cheered the arrival of a 27-foot sculpture modeled after the Statue of Liberty.

Reversing their earlier position, thousands of university students resolved on Monday to maintain pressure on the Government by continuing their round-the-clock occupation of Tiananmen Square for at least three more weeks.

In an emotional scene at the square in the heart of Beijing late Monday night, a crowd of nearly 100,000 workers and students cheered the arrival of a 27-foot sculpture modeled after the Statue of Liberty. The statue, made by local art students and dragged to the square in several pieces on tricycle carts, was called the Goddess of Democracy and Freedom, to distinguish it from the Statue of Liberty in New York Harbor.

The exuberance was a reminder of some of the students' past triumphs in rallying large numbers of people around the nation to support their demands for a more democratic system and less corruption. In recent days, the movement seems to have slumped from a combination of weariness and uncertainty about how to respond to the rise of a hard-line faction in power struggles within the Communist Party leadership.

New Mood of Defiance

With the number of students occupying the square slipping steadily, student leaders on Saturday had called for a retreat to the university campuses. But on Monday, displaying a new mood of defiance, most of the students remaining on the square declared that to leave would be an admission of defeat. They resolved to stay at least until a meeting of the standing committee of the National People's Congress on June 20.

The tens of thousands of students occupying Tiananmen Square at the height of the demonstrations has dwindled to fewer than 10,000, and the lack of garbage collection has left it increasingly dirty and foul smelling. Most Beijing area students have already left, so that those remaining are from other parts of China. The students' occupation of the square is in its third week.

The decision to remain in the square, and the arrival of the statue, seemed to raise the protesters' spirits and create a new sense of the possibilities of the movement.

"She signifies hope for China," said Y.H. Yang, a 22-year-old teacher who was in the crowd. "But she's behind schedule in reaching the square, and she's coming by tricycle. That is symbolic of the slowness and backwardness of the democratization process in China."

Public Relations Coup Seen

It was not clear how the Government would react to makeshift monument, one that dominates the eye of anyone traveling along the capital's main east-west thoroughfare, the Avenue of Eternal Peace. Officials will probably be tempted to take it away, but the students say that the only way to dismantle it would be to smash it. The statue is made of plaster and plastic foam.

The students regard the statue as a public relations coup: either it will remain and symbolize the democracy movement and official weakness; or the authorities will be in the embarrassing position of sending the police to attack the Goddess of Democracy and Freedom with sledgehammers.

By naming the statue a goddess, the students win a little extra cachet for their creation. Chinese folk beliefs

Tiananmen Square's plaster and plastic foam "Goddess of Democracy and Freedom" was modeled after the Statue of Liberty and symbolized the hope for democracy across China. (**AP Images.**)

include a pantheon of gods, from the Kitchen God to the God of Fishermen.

Goddess with Caucasian Face

On the other hand, the Goddess closely resembles the Statue of Liberty, to the point of having Caucasian features and a large Western nose. A few spectators said they thought it might have been more appropriate for her to have Chinese features, but nobody seemed too concerned about such particulars.

"We don't care if she resembles Westerners or Chinese," said T.X. Wang, a 29-year-old factory worker. "The most important thing is that she symbolizes our common hopes for democracy."

Perhaps because many of the fainter-hearted students already have left, the mood on Tiananmen Square now is markedly more resolute than just a few days ago. The students have cleaned up the square to some extent, and they insisted that they would remain indefinitely.

"Tiananmen Square has become a symbol of democracy in China," said Chen Di, a 23-year-old student from Shenyang. "We can't abandon it."

Arrivals and Departures

Mr. Chen's classmate Liu Gang interjected: "If we left, the student movement would certainly lose. And if we stay, the Government will be forced to make a choice. Either it will agree to a dialogue with students, or it will stage a crackdown. And if it chooses the crackdown, it will lose support."

Most of the students acknowledge that most of the students will drift away in the coming days and weeks, but some say that new ones will come and take their places. Each day hundreds of new students arrive to join the sit-in at Tiananmen Square, but for now even larger numbers are leaving the capital each day.

As the movement's momentum has waned, local residents who had heaped food and blankets on the demonstrators seemed to be cutting back on their material support. Still, offerings of sustenance continued.

"The students are patriotic, and we must support them," said Xue Yuhai, a 74-year-old fruit seller who had just bicycled over with several tubs of food to give to the students. "We'll continue to give contributions as long as there are students here."

One of China's retired leaders lent his support Monday to Prime Minister Li Peng in his power struggle with the Communist Party leader, Zhao Ziyang. Peng Zhen, the former head of the National People's Congress, supported Mr. Li's military crackdown against the democracy movement and without naming anyone he seemed to attack Mr. Zhao by criticizing "the very small number of conspirators and bad elements who took advantage of the situation to create turmoil."

Still, Mr. Peng's speech was not as hard line as might have been expected, since he is regarded as one of the retired leaders most suspicious of rapid liberalization.

The World Reacts to News of the Tiananmen Square Crackdown

Robert D. McFadden

In the following selection, *New York Times* reporter Robert D. McFadden writes of responses on the parts of various governments and of overseas Chinese to the news that the Chinese government had used its army to shoot protesters in and around Tiananmen Square on June 4, 1989. Governments of many Western countries, he notes, clearly condemned the measures, while the Communist Soviet Union and some Asian countries were more measured or cautious in their reactions. Overseas Chinese communities, meanwhile, often staged large protest demonstrations. Some of the biggest were in Hong Kong and Macao, then British and Portuguese colonies, respectively, where the majority Chinese populations would within 10 years find themselves under direct Chinese authority. Chinese university students in the United States, for their part, gathered in major cities such as New York, Chicago, and San Francisco

SOURCE. Robert D. McFadden, "The West Condemns the Crackdown," *The New York Times*, June 5, 1989. Copyright © 1989 by The New York Times Company. Reproduced by permission.

to stage rallies of their own, and some visited the Chinese Embassy in Washington, D.C., to make their feelings known.

Western nations and Chinese around the world condemned the military crackdown and bloodshed in Beijing yesterday with anguished protests, pleas for restraint and calls for economic and political sanctions against China.

The United States, Britain, France, West Germany, Italy, Spain, the Netherlands and Sweden all issued statements deploring the shooting of hundreds of demonstrators by the Chinese Army. Pope John Paul II, in Finland, expressed hope that the tragedy would lead to positive changes in China.

The Soviet Union did not comment on the events in China. Moscow television spoke of Beijing as "a frontline city," but gave only sketchy accounts of casualties and did not mention that tanks had been used to attack pro-democracy demonstrators. Polish television carried witness reports of the killings from Tiananmen Square.

China's Asian neighbors were slower to react, but Chinese students and other protesters marched tearfully and angrily in Hong Kong, Macao and Taipei as well as in Paris, London, Oslo and Vancouver and in many cities across the United States.

Up to 200,000 people joined demonstrations in Hong Kong, where fears have run high in anticipation of the transition to Chinese sovereignty in 1997. As many as 150,000 people—a quarter of the population—were involved in protests in the Portuguese colony of Macao, and 10,000 more rallied in Taipei.

> Many protesters and public officials said the Beijing Government had lost its legitimacy.

Western Denunciations

President Bush denounced China for using military force against its own

people and implied that the action could damage relations between Washington and Beijing. Prime Minister Margaret Thatcher of Britain said she was "appalled by the indiscriminate shooting of unarmed people."

The French Foreign Minister, Roland Dumas, said he was "dismayed by the bloody repression" of "an unarmed crowd of demonstrators." The West German Foreign Ministry urged China "to return to its universally welcomed policies of reform and openness." The Netherlands and Sweden also deplored the bloodshed.

While statements by President Bush, Prime Minister Thatcher and other Western leaders were forceful, it was the anguish etched on the faces of ordinary people—many of them with relatives in China—that captured the depth of emotions unleashed by the weekend massacre of Chinese people by their own Government.

"Sometimes, I thought I would go back and help my country," said a 29-year-old graduate student at Long Island University who attended one of several rallies in New York City. "But I don't think there's any hope at this moment."

Other demonstrators, outrage visible behind the sobs, compared the leaders of their homeland to Hitler and spoke of Prime Minister Li Peng as a murderer. Some raised Chinese flags that had been spray-painted with Nazi swastikas.

Calls for End to Arms Aid

Many protesters and public officials said the Beijing Government had lost its legitimacy and no longer deserved the people's support. Some predicted the fall of the Government and called for political isolation of China. Others urged economic sanctions that could damage China's economy through a loss of tourism, trade and investments.

Senator Paul Simon, an Illinois Democrat, urged President Bush to suspend military aid to China and

Photo on previous page: People in New York's Chinatown took to the streets on June 10, 1989 to demonstrate against Beijing's response to the Tiananmen Square protests. (AP Images.)

to work with American allies to suspend economic aid. Representative Bill Paxon of New York urged Mr. Bush to recall the American Ambassador and to consider imposing economic sanctions.

Weeping and chanting, wearing emblems of mourning, carrying banners and placards denouncing the Beijing Government leaders, thousands of Chinese students and Chinese Americans rallied and marched in New York, Washington, Los Angeles, San Francisco, Chicago, Houston, New Orleans and other cities. No violence was reported at any of the protests.

In New York, where one of the biggest protests unfolded, 6,000 demonstrators marched across Manhattan from the Chinese Consulate on 42d Street and 12th Avenue to the United Nations. "We don't recognize the Government," said Qiang Peng, a University of Rhode Island student from Beijing. Many protesters were from colleges across the Northeast.

Some marchers wore T-shirts emblazoned with "Democracy in China," and black arm bands mourning their dead countrymen. Others bore signs declaring: "Punish the Slaughterers," and "Drown the Dictators with Our Blood." Among the chants was one that applauded Zhao Ziyang, the moderate Communist Party leader, who has dropped out of sight.

Other Protests in New York

Elsewhere in New York, there were other protests. At Columbia University, about 1,000 Chinese students heard a series of impassioned speeches condemning the Beijing Government. And 400 people rallied at Confucius Plaza in Chinatown; many signed postcards urging Mr. Bush to "take immediate diplomatic and political measures" against China.

> In Chicago, 6,000 people from 35 universities in the Middle West marched in a mock funeral procession to mourn the Beijing dead.

In Chicago, 6,000 people from 35 universities in the Middle West marched in a mock funeral procession to mourn the Beijing dead. They demanded the resignations of Mr. Li and China's senior leader, Deng Xiaoping, and extensive reforms of the Chinese Communist Party. Senator Simon urged Congress to consider a resolution condemning China.

Rallying outside the Chinese Embassy in Washington, 3,000 protesters—many of them from universities in the East, South and Middle West who rode in cars and buses all night to take part—demanded that the Chinese Ambassador to the United States, Han Xu, and other officials come out and justify their Government's actions.

"Why don't they come out?" one protester roared over a bullhorn. "Are they ashamed? They hide like mice from us, from democracy."

Two Chinese students from Penn State University tried to present a huge mourning wreath at the front door for those killed in Beijing, but they were turned away by security guards. The embassy shades remained drawn all day, although a man was seen in an upper-story window taking photographs of the protesters.

In San Francisco, about 3,000 people gathered outside the Chinese Consulate with banners in Chinese and English proclaiming: "Students Are Bleeding and We Are Weeping," and "Blood Must Atone for Blood." Marching later to City Hall and through Chinatown, they also carried poster caricatures of Mr. Deng and Mr. Li in fascist garb.

There's No Longer Any Hope

"Two weeks ago, we still had some illusions," said David Chien, an engineer. "Now, there's no longer any hope unless the Government steps down." Behind him on the side of the consulate, spray-painted in red were the words: "Remember Beijing Massacre, June 4, 1989."

In Los Angeles, more than 1,000 protesters assembled outside the Chinese Consulate to decry the violence in Beijing, express support for the Chinese democracy movement and demand the ouster of the Communist Government. The demonstrators also called on the United States to take a strong stand against the violence.

"They shouldn't use guns and tanks," said Ming Tan, a former University of Arizona student from Shanghai. "Those are weapons for war."

About 1,000 Chinese students and others from Texas and nearby states gathered in Houston and marched to the Chinese Consulate for an orderly but angry protest in 88-degree heat. Two representatives of the protest were allowed inside to speak to the Consul General, Yao Xianni, but he declined to address the crowd.

About 650 Chinese students and Chinese Americans held an emotional rally near Independence Hall in Philadelphia. Other protests took place over the weekend in Seattle, New Orleans, St. Paul and Buffalo.

Tiananmen Square Was the Flashpoint of a Nationwide Movement

Michael Fathers and Andrew Higgins

The following selection was compiled and written by Michael Fathers and Andrew Higgins, reporters for the British newspaper *The Independent*. Fathers and Higgins were in China during the Tiananmen Square protests and the violent crackdowns that ended them. While events in Beijing received a great deal of news attention, Fathers and Higgins make it clear that student protests occurred throughout China, as did government violence and arrests in response to them. Among the locations where protests took place was the major city of Shanghai, where protesters built a small model of the Statue of Liberty, a move later followed in Tiananmen Square. In China's far southern city of Guangzhou, not far from the then-British colony of Hong Kong, students at one point launched a hunger strike, another gesture of protest also made in Beijing.

SOURCE. Michael Fathers and Andrew Higgins, *Tiananmen: The Rape of Peking*. London: The Independent/Doubleday, 1989. Copyright © 1989 Newspaper Publishing plc, Michael Fathers, Andrew Higgins and Robert Cottrell. Reproduced by permission.

Guangdong. On the evening of May 4 [1989], police tried unsuccessfully to halt a demonstration in Canton [Guangzhou] by thousands of students from Zhongshan University, Jinan University and Huannan Teacher's University. On May 16, another street procession was staged. The next day, a sit-in and 24-hour hunger strike [were] launched in front of the headquarters of the provincial government. By May 18, the crowd had swelled to 30,000. On June 4, students occupied the Haizhou Bridge in Canton for one hour. The next day, they returned to block traffic at so many key locations as to bring the city to a standstill, and paralyzed the railway system by lying on the tracks at Tianhe District. On June 6, 19 "hooligans" were briefly arrested. The provincial government announced new regulations against unofficial bodies, and set up a special discipline and inspection unit for colleges. By June 27, students had returned to class.

> "The provincial government . . . set up a special discipline and inspection unit for colleges."

Hubei. The seriousness of events in Hubei could be judged from a notice [that] appeared after order had been restored. It threatened action against ringleaders who had been "collecting crowds to storm party and government organs and factories, mines and enterprises, and to block traffic and disrupt social order, resulting in the cutting of road and railway traffic, and criminal elements who took part in smashing, looting and burning. "Over half" the city's students were officially regarded as having been involved in the unrest.

On April 28, the province's deputy party secretary urged a "clear-cut stand" against disorder. On May 16, students began a sit-in at one end of a bridge over the Yangtze River at Wuhan, bringing heavy traffic to a standstill. On May 22, the city was placed under control of the military police. They used pepper, tear gas and cattle prods to disperse crowds. . . .

On June 4, students staged a sit-in to block tracks on Wuchang bridge. In the following week, police began arresting activists. On June 7, they reported detaining "criminal elements." On June 10, the public security bureau said it had arrested 28 "unemployed and disreputable workers" who had been shouting slogans and harassing passers-by. On June 11, most students returned to their classes. On June 15, the Wuhan College Students' Autonomous Federation was officially banned. Newspapers were advised to "improve their management."

Hunan. Hunan was [reformist Chinese political leader] Hu Yaobang's home province. The response to his death was severe. As early as April 22, incidents of beating, smashing and looting were reported on the streets of Changsha. Nine people were arrested in connection with this riot a week later. On May 4, about 2,000 students demonstrated. On May 17, many times that number came together to support the Peking [Beijing] hunger strike. About 10,000 congregated at the main railway station. Tens of thousands more students, teachers, journalists and blue-collar workers took to the streets the next day.

> Three Americans were expelled, accused of impersonating students.

Rallies of this magnitude continued for at least another week, focused on a sit-in outside the provincial government headquarters which lasted until May 29. On May 23, four foreign teachers said that they saw more than 40 students and workers being beaten up at the bridge by at least three truckloads of soldiers. After the Peking massacre, protestors brought the city to a standstill. The chaos lasted at least until June 9, when the mayor of Changsha appealed for order. Two days later, the public security bureau had arrested at least 31 "rioters." On June 15, police searched nine publishing

Shanghai protest- ers' re-creation of the Statue of Liberty inspired students elsewhere, including ones at Tiananmen Square. (**AP Images.**)

houses believed to have printed "counter-revolutionary" material.

Shaanxi. Residents of Xian gathered to mourn Hu Yaobang on April 19. On April 22, the day of his funeral, riots broke out. Ten vehicles and twenty houses were burnt. At Xincheng Square, 130 armed police were reported injured. Police trucks [infested] the town. On April 26, police said they were making arrests. Students at the Northwestern Industrial University received permission to demonstrate on the streets on May 4. On May 17, they petitioned for a meeting with the governor, and began a hunger strike, calling for the "truth" about the April 22 disturbance to be "clarified."

On May 20, Xian was brought to a standstill as 300,000 protestors took to the streets. Students occupied the central square, and showed pictures which they said illustrated police brutality on April 22. Demonstrations continued in the square until May 28, when students returned to school. On June 3, three Americans were expelled, accused of impersonating students.

> The arrests of 'ruffians' and 'criminals' accelerated.

On June 10–11, the provincial Party issued a series of orders. It banned autonomous workers' and students' unions, and the production of "reactionary slogans." On June 12, 43 "saboteurs" were arrested; on June 13, 75 "lawbreakers," including student leaders.

Shanghai. The first reported demonstration took place in the early hours of April 20, five days after Hu's death. Several hundred students marched to the municipal government headquarters on Waitan—the Bund [Shanghai's main public thoroughfare]—and were later joined by large crowds of onlookers. The city's Party boss, Jiang Zemin, complained on April 26 about the appearance of big character posters around university campuses. The first large daytime demonstration took place on May 2, when 6,000 students marched from their colleges to People's Square in the centre of the city. On May 4, about 5,000 students marched again to People's Square, where they began a sit-in outside the municipal government headquarters; on May 16, 4,000 students and young teachers decided to stage their own hunger strike in sympathy with Peking. On May 17–18 the protests multiplied in size to embrace all sectors of the society. Cadres paraded alongside students and workers. On May 20, two days after [Soviet leader] Mikhail Gorbachev's stopover, the students placed a small model of the Statue of Liberty outside the government headquarters, which probably served as the inspiration for the more dramatic "Goddess of Democracy," produced by the Central Institute of Fine Art for erection on Tiananmen Square a week later.

A mass march on May 28 signalled the onset of worse disruption, reaching near-chaos after the June 3–4 Peking massacre. Crowds sat in on railway tracks leading into the city centre, and on June 6 demonstrators blocking the line at Guangxin junction were mown down by a train. At least six were killed, and as many again injured. The crowd set fire to the train. By now, the official crackdown was underway. On June 9, nine members of the Autonomous Workers' Union were arrested. On June 10, the municipal police said they had uncovered two "counter-revolutionary cliques," the China Youth Democratic Party and the Freedom Society, and repeated their declaration that unofficial student organizations were illegal. That same day, the police made ten arrests in connection with the June 6 assault on the train. The next day, they detained a Hong Kong student, Yao Yongzhan, accusing him of being involved with illegal activities, and expelled a British journalist, Peter Newport.

The arrests of "ruffians" and "criminals" accelerated. By June 13, 166 had been reported. On June 15, three of those arrested for firing the train were sentenced to death—the first publicized use of the death penalty in connection with the democracy movement. On June 21, the executions were carried out.

Sichuan. On April 19, "many people" were said to be mourning Hu Yaobang, who had close ties with

Sichuan. . . . On April 20, students demonstrated in the centre of Chengdu. The next day, they staged a memorial service for Hu on Renmin Nanlu Square. Sporadic demonstrations continued, focused on a sit-in on the square. On May 17, the provincial vice-governor agreed to meet students the following day. Many students were trying to board trains to Peking. By June 1, protestors were blockading main roads around Chengdu. One was killed and five injured when a goods vehicle crashed into a blockade.

On June 4, Chengdu's main department store was burnt down. Radio reports said the crowd also burnt a police station and fire engines, which tried to intervene. Police were attacked with stones and bottles. The next day saw further intense violence. A Japanese visitor claimed that 300 students were killed, and a thousand injured. An attempt was made to burn the Jinjiang Hotel, which housed the US consulate. On June 6, further disturbances were reported; and also 100 arrests.

The authorities were beginning to crack down. On June 10, "criminals" were called upon to surrender. On June 14, autonomous organizations were banned. Chengdu police made 106 arrests on June 19; and on July 18, two "counter-revolutionaries" were executed.

Most of the Victims of June 1989 Died Outside Tiananmen Square

Robert Marquand

Following the Tiananmen Square crackdown on the night of June 3–4, 1989, the outside world came to believe that the protests had ended with a massacre of students in the square ordered by the Chinese government and carried out by the People's Liberation Army (PLA). But while some students died in the square, most of the actual victims of the crackdown died in Beijing's streets, outside Tiananmen Square. These victims were not students but ordinary people who resented the government's heavy-handed treatment of the students or who got caught up in events.

In the following selection, journalist Robert Marquand, writing on the fifteenth anniversary of the crackdown, summarizes his examination of the events of June 3 and 4. He suggests that

---

SOURCE. Robert Marquand, "New Story Emerges of an Infamous Massacre," *Christian Science Monitor*, June 3, 2004. Copyright © 2004 The Christian Science Publishing Society. All rights reserved. Reproduced by permission from *Christian Science Monitor*. (www .csmonitor.com).

there are no credible eyewitness accounts of a massacre in the square. Instead, the students appeared to negotiate an agreement to leave the square, which they did in the early morning hours of June 4, marching together past the PLA's guns. Those who were killed died over the next hours and days, and were likely among the hundreds of thousands who had come to Beijing to demonstrate their support for the student protests. Robert Marquand is a staff writer for the *Christian Science Monitor*.

> A massacre did take place in Beijing 15 years ago . . . just not in Tiananmen.

On the 15th anniversary of one of the most cataclysmic events in modern China, a wealth of eyewitness testimony and interviews suggest that one stubbornly popular picture of what happened in Tiananmen Square needs revision: There was no massacre of students on the Square.

Standard histories such as that by Yale's Jonathan Spence, as well as the recent groundbreaking "Tiananmen Papers," suggest that Chinese soldiers did not fire on students before they left the square in the early hours of June 4, 1989. But in popular references, most recently in the first paragraph of a major retrospective wire story this week stating that "thousands were killed in Tiananmen Square," the myth persists. A massacre did take place in Beijing 15 years ago, eyewitnesses say—just not in Tiananmen.

What is famously known as the June 4 massacre actually began on the evening of June 3. The night was cool and windless, eyewitnesses remember. The student uprising that shocked China's leadership with calls for democratic reform, and that captured the attention of the world, was nine weeks old by then.

One exhausted protest leader remembers retiring at 10:15 P.M. on June 3 in one of hundreds of makeshift tents in the square—unaware, in a pre-cellphone era, that Army columns were already rolling in on a westerly road.

Many journalists and observers had earlier strolled three blocks to the Beijing Hotel for a relaxed dinner. By June 3, in fact, the Tiananmen story seemed in a lull, and many reporters were pulled back to Tokyo or Hong Kong. Just weeks earlier, 2 million people were arriving each day to China's most sacred public site. They were reacting to the imposition of martial law and the dismissal of reform leader Zhao Ziyang, who was sympathetic to the students, and who among other things appeared to favor the policy of *glasnost* [openness] that was changing the Soviet Union.

Yet by June 3 the numbers were down; the students were tired and squabbling.

Rumors and Reality

Rumors came of an Army crackdown. But such rumors had swirled for weeks. Most students on the square at this point were not the original cast from the elite colleges of Beijing. These protesters had come from the provinces. Some arriving June 3 said they wanted to contribute to a "new China, less corrupt."

Few observers were prepared for what happened next.

In two hours, between midnight and 2 A.M., the slightly riotous, unorganized festival of meetings and exhilarated free speech on the square became a grim confrontation with an Army that surrounded the students, and was using live rounds against citizens in neighborhoods all over the city.

> What actually did happen . . . is still often confused with myth and misreporting.

That night still lives in infamy to many who remember it. Chinese leaders remain silent about the event 15 years later. No mistakes have been admitted nor has any government accounting been done. In today's bustling

Many who died after the Tiananmen Square protests on June 4, 1989 were not students but ordinary citizens who supported the goals of the would-be reformers. (**AP Images.**)

commercial China, moreover, few speak of the brutal putdown. New generations here profess lack of interest in the question of who was and wasn't a patriot, or what transpired, not that there are any rewards for such curiosity.

What actually did happen June 3–4 is still often confused with myth and misreporting.

Early wire reports, including a second-day account by a Tsinghua student, now widely regarded as disinformation, and several assertions to the media by student leaders who were not present, planted some of the misconceptions that persist today. A British reporter (who left the square at 1:30 P.M.) for example, wrote a widely read account based entirely on secondhand sources who claimed a massacre took place in the square.

In fact, the panic was so intense that most impartial observers left the square by midnight. In those days, says one European journalist who was there, "no one ever believed that the Army would actually shoot people."

As few as 10 foreigners actually witnessed events on the square during the crucial early morning hours of June 4, according to eyewitnesses interviewed by the *Monitor*, and an unpublished 52-page document compiled entirely in the weeks after by Robin Munro (then of Human Rights Watch) and Richard Nations (a *Le Monde* reporter) of 14 testimonials of journalists, diplomats, and students present on the square after midnight.

> The victims were not only students, but ordinary people who were outraged that the soldiers of a people's army had been given warrant to shoot the people.

No Eyewitnesses to a Massacre

Despite orders that the People's Liberation Army was to clear Tiananmen Square using whatever means necessary, there is no credible eyewitness testimony of a massacre of students there. No eyewitnesses at the Monument to the People's Heroes, where students were centered, ever saw one. No "rivers of blood" flowed on the square. No rows of students were mowed down by a sudden rush of troops, as reported in European, Hong Kong, and U.S. publications in the days, months, and years that followed.

The actual number of students and citizens killed on the square may be as low as a dozen, according to the documents and the eyewitnesses. The medical tent on the square, originally used to comfort student hunger strikers, reported at least 10 deaths. Rather, between the morning hours of 4:45 and 6:15, some 2,000 to 3,000 students filed off the square through a cordon of troops, protected by a line of their own ranks who linked arms.

There was, however, a massacre in Beijing—during the four days starting June 3. It took place at street intersections, in Hutong [side-street] neighborhoods, in the alleyways around the square, and in the western part of the city, where resistance to the deployment of the Army was strongest. Moreover, the victims were not only students, but ordinary people who were outraged that the soldiers of a people's army had been given warrant to shoot the people.

An Outraged Beijing Population

One emerging interpretation of the June 4 event is that the students avoided a massacre—partly, and symbolically, by using their power to vote.

By 4 A.M. on the square, one of the most dangerous moments had arrived. In testimony compiled by Mr. Munro, and including Mr. Nations, and Juan Restrepro of Spanish TV, among others—all of whom stayed with the students until they left the square—matters had by then reached a "lethal" tension point. Soldiers surrounded the students from three sides—at the Forbidden City, Great Hall of the People, and the History Museum. The square was lighted. Some 2,000 students huddled at the towering monument at center square. They sang the [Communist anthem] "Internationale," with its verse, "the final battle is upon us, unite until the morrow." Orange flames from burning tents leapt up.

Students wore headbands that said "ready to die." Military loudspeakers competed with student loudspeakers. Students urged each other to, "Keep order, stay calm. We must not give them a pretext [to shoot.]" At one point about 4:15 the lights on the square went out and some 10,000 People's Liberation Army troops ran out of the entrance of the Great Hall in what seemed an attempt to frighten students into scattering. But they remained poised.

What happened instead, according to Munro's account, was a kind of surreal debate at a moment of decision. The head of the Peking students autonomous federation urged all students to stay and face the guns.

"We will now pay the highest price possible, for the sake of securing democracy for China. Our blood will be the consecration," are his words in Munro's notes. Yet immediately leader Hou Dejian disagreed, saying on the loudspeaker: "We have already won a great victory. But now we have to go."

The minutes ticked by and no actions were taken. Munro says, "My gut feeling was that everyone present knew perfectly well why they were there; it was a private conviction but one that all shared."

Square Standoff Decided by Vote

It appeared that they might stay. But in what seemed an afterthought, someone, it is not clear who, came on the speaker to suggest taking a vote. "It was . . . at the time a stroke of genius" that may have saved thousands of lives, Munro recalled.

Between 5 and 6 A.M. the students left the memorial and filed out to the southwest part of the square, walking behind the banners that marked which college they were from.

"There was absolutely no one killed at the Monument [of the People's Heroes]," said Spanish cameraman Rodriques, who was filming the entire evening, and whose testimony contrasts with 15 years of unattributed rumor. "Everyone left and no one was killed."

"Student leaders had pulled off the most difficult maneuver . . . an orderly retreat," Richard Nations said in testimony given weeks later. "The real violence still lay ahead but at that moment the 1989 democratic movement was over, and the next phase began as the column walked off the theater of national politics at Tiananmen."

Mr. Restrepro was on hand as the students departed past a Kentucky Fried Chicken shop: At daybreak "It was one of those extraordinary moments. . . . The students were carrying their banners. . . . Some had no shoes. I shall remember this for the rest of my life, the faces of those boys and girls. . . . At 5 A.M. the first flags coming out . . . and it took one hour . . . and as they [left] the people began insulting the soldiers and cheering . . . the students. Then some began to throw stones . . . and it was dangerous."

Residents Aid the Students

One dynamic that eyewitnesses say played a central role was the relationship between students and ordinary Beijing people. By late May the common people were very impressed, if not a bit smitten with what they called "our" students. By the end of May, as the students tested their resolve through hunger strikes, workers and citizens were sending them water, offering help with sanitation and medical supplies, and giving general tender loving care.

"The people loved the students because they could see the students loved China," one schoolteacher who lived near the square remembers now. "That was the thing. We didn't think of them as anticommunist. We could see they were patriots who were for democracy. But after June 4, we could no longer say this."

On June 3 as the Army began approaching the square about midnight—calls went out all over Beijing. Sympathetic crowds numbering in the tens of thousands felt the Army was coming to shoot the students. There are hundreds of accounts of citizens, mothers and sons alike, chasing tanks in bicycles, setting fire to trucks, putting up road blocks. At the Jianguomenwai overpass a set of locals talked an entire truckful of soldiers into climbing down. But the price paid by the citizens was high, as the troops—many of whom were brought into Beijing from all over China—began to retaliate.

"By June, the ordinary people identified with the students 100 percent," Munro remembers. "Beijing people are outraged when the soldiers leave their barracks. They said the soldiers planned to kill 'our' students, as they put it."

The bulk of departing students who left the square in a column took several turns and eventually crossed the Avenue of Eternal Peace just west of Tiananmen. At that point, one of the worst incidents involving students took place, as APCs [armored personnel carriers] fired on and ran over at least 11 students. AP reporter John Pomfret, traveling in the column, saw students remove seven bodies, and soldiers began to shoot tear gas into the student ranks, according to the Munro-collected testimony. . . .

A number of later discredited accounts of a "massacre" in the square came out in the days following June 4. Student leader Wuer Kaixi claimed "2,000 perished" and claimed to have seen two rows of students killed, though it is later shown he left the square about 4 A.M.

A Hong Kong student leader was quoted as saying "a thousand" were killed, but later admits under questioning that he has actually seen no killings.

Roderick MacFarquhar, a history professor at Harvard University, says the estimates of the final death toll range from 800 to 1,000. But, one eyewitness in Beijing who later wrote a book on Chinese nationalism points out that the actual numbers or locations are not crucial 15 years later. "Whether the figure is 900 or 2,052, is not the issue," he says.

"We don't want to start bargaining with the lives of victims. What now matters is a serious confession that it happened, and then an accounting of what happened. That's what we still don't have."

The Tiananmen Square Crackdown Was a Key Moment in Modern China's Development

Jonathan Fenby

In the following selection, British journalist Jonathan Fenby makes the argument that, with the Tiananmen Square crackdown, Chinese leaders were demonstrating that modern China was following a path of development that both echoed ancient traditions and reflected the industrialized, consumerist world of the late twentieth and early twenty-first centuries. He claims that the crackdown remains an important symbol of this state of development despite its relatively small number of victims. As Fenby notes, millions died of hunger when, in the Great Leap Forward of the late 1950s, Communist China tried to

SOURCE. Jonathan Fenby, "Remembering Tiananmen: The Massacre in Beijing, 19 Years Ago Today, Is Officially a Nonevent but Was a Crucial Moment in China's History," *Guardian (UK)*, June 4, 2008. Copyright © 2008 Guardian Newspapers Limited. Reproduced by permission of Guardian News Service, LTD.

industrialize quickly and haphazardly. Thousands also perished during the Cultural Revolution of 1966–1976, when Communist hard-liners sought unsuccessfully to destroy China's history and traditions.

With Tiananmen Square, Fenby argues, Chinese leaders were signaling that order and stability were desirable virtues, even in an economy that was modernizing and liberalizing rapidly. Furthermore, order and stability had to be imposed from the top down, by a single, unified governing authority, as they were in earlier eras of Chinese history. According to Fenby, China's government remained in this "Beijing coma" even as of his writing the selection in 2008. Jonathan Fenby was editor of the British newspaper *Observer* as well as of Hong Kong's *South China Morning Post*.

F or some, the events that occurred in Beijing 19 years ago today [June 4, 2008] have been pushed towards the sidelines of history.

The Great Leap Forward [late 1950s] and the consequent famine or the 10 years of the Cultural Revolution [1965–75] were, in purely quantitative terms, much longer and bigger (including in terms of victims) than the massacre of protesters on the night of June 3–4, 1989.

Besides the economic expansion of the last decades, the Beijing Spring can all too easily take on the aura of a carnival which ended in tragedy and, basically, led nowhere. [London Mayor] Ken Livingstone compared it to the poll tax riot in London [in 1990], and "friends" of China take care to describe it as the Tiananmen Incident or, at most, as a "clampdown". The protesters have been suppressed or forced into exile across the globe, except for those who have come to terms with the regime that rules in the new China; a few are still in prison.

What happened that night is a non-event as far as the rulers of China are concerned; commemoration is suppressed and, if it is remembered at all, the occasion is portrayed as a glorious defence of the people's true interests by the army. How many people died remains unknown, though what is clear is that most were not students in Tiananmen, but ordinary citizens of the capital trying to stop the armoured vehicles after previous successes at blocking their progress to the square.

> If the Chinese were to be free to run their lives economically, why not politically as well?

Yet June 4 remains a crucial moment in China's history, as I have sought to show in a new history of China that seeks to link past and present. The killings of June 4 were enough of a tragedy in themselves. But, beyond the deaths along the boulevard leading to Tiananmen and then in the square, the outcome of the Beijing Spring confirmed China

The Cultural Revolution

From 1966 to 1976 Chinese life was dominated by a political struggle known as the Great Proletarian Cultural Revolution. The event is generally understood as an attempt by Mao Zedong to reassert his authority over the larger "revolutionary" movement then bringing communism to China. By 1966, Mao was losing influence to such men as Deng Xiaoping and Liu Shaoqi, leaders who favored economic and political reforms. With the help of supporters such as Lin Biao and his wife Jiang Qing, Mao was able to marginalize Deng and Liu and fill China's leading political committee with a so-called Cultural Revolution Group. This group pronounced itself ready to revere Mao and so-called "Mao Zedong thought" and to return revolutionary fervor to China's people.

Much of the work of the Cultural Revolution was carried out by groups of young people known as Red Guards whose leaders, especially, were filled with revolutionary enthusiasm. During the Red Guards' campaign to overthrow the "Four Olds" of old ideas, old customs, old habits, and old traditions, these young people destroyed or defaced many ancient monuments and other historical treasures. They also in a political course which reaches back into distant history, but from which, crucially, Deng Xiaoping and his elderly colleagues decided not to divert 19 years ago.

The patriarch, the ultimate survivor of the Communist system, embarked on the path of economic, market-led reform in 1978 after his victory over [Communist China's founder] Mao's anointed successor, Hua Guofeng. While this was hugely successful in one sense, kick-starting the moribund economy and bringing China into the world economic system, it had, by 1989, aroused widespread resentment bred from the inequality Deng saw as necessary for growth, inflation and corruption.

> The desire . . . for a peaceful way forward . . . has little or no place in a tradition that . . . puts a premium on top-down rule.

attacked, mostly verbally but sometimes physically, those whose ideas or behavior were too "bourgeois," or middle-class. These victims included their teachers and parents. Meanwhile, millions of Chinese "intellectuals," meaning those with educations, were sent into the countryside to work in agriculture in Mao's "down to the countryside" movement while thousands of political dissidents were imprisoned or even executed.

By the early 1970s Mao Zedong's health was declining, but the Cultural Revolution was carried on by a group of hardliners known as the "Gang of Four:" Jiang Qing, Zhang Chunqiao, Yao Wenyuan, and Wang Yongwen. In China's inner circle of power they were opposed by such figures as Zhou Enlai and Deng Xiaoping, the latter returned to a position of importance in 1974. Zhou was very popular among China's citizens, and his death in early 1976 inspired huge public outpourings of sympathy. The Gang of Four proved unable to surmount the public support for Zhou's faction. Following the death of Mao himself in September 1976, the Gang of Four were arrested and the Cultural Revolution officially over.

But there was a more fundamental question: if the Chinese were to be free to run their lives economically, why not politically as well? If the command economy was being dismantled, why not the command political system, too?

The student demonstrators in the square may have lacked a coherent message. The atmosphere may have taken on aspects of a carnival. But, underlying it all was a basic questioning of the right of the Communist Party to exercise monopoly power, a demand for discussion and plurality.

A Relic of China's District Past

That questioned a tenet of Chinese rule dating back to the First Emperor of 221 B.C. The doctrine of legalism—rule by law rather than rule of law—co-existed with the more benevolent strains of Confucianism. Mao had identified himself with the First Emperor, and in 1980, Deng and his colleagues were in no mood to cede the authority they had spent all their lives fighting for.

> People are . . . far freer than they were under Mao, so long as they are not seen to represent any political threat.

Their decision to declare martial law and send in the People's Liberation Army was not taken lightly. As shown in the smuggled-out records in the book, *The Tiananmen Papers*, they deliberated long and hard, often in deep disgruntlement as they discussed how to deal with the pesky students who could draw on the traditional esteem in which their class was held in China. Reformists in the leadership, led by the party secretary, Zhao Ziyang, tried to find an accommodation. By the beginning of June, some student leaders were ready to return to campus and build on the moral victory they had won since launching the protest in mid-April. But the moderates were overruled on both sides and the tragic result unfolded.

That may say something about the dynamics of a student movement that was poorly co-ordinated and lacked clear, realisable aims—and was filled with its fair share of egos and hot-heads. But it says a lot more about the Chinese leadership, then and since. The desire for compromise, for understanding, for a peaceful way forward that encompasses as many participants as possible has little or no place in a tradition that, stretching back through the imperial millennia, puts a premium on top-down rule with force always lurking in the background to be used on dissidents who are portrayed as traitors to the received wisdom exercised by the rulers. Against that, the moderates, were they Zhao or the student leader Wang Dan, could not make reason prevail.

Authority Rather Than Compromise

Gathered in Deng's house as they circumvented the constitution and Zhao Ziyang to impose their will, the elders convinced themselves that the students must be manipulated by foreign enemies and "black hands" operating clandestinely in Beijing—some of those who tried to mediate a settlement found themselves cast into that category and sentenced to long prison terms. The Mandate of Heaven [an old Chinese idea suggesting that the heavens approve of leaders as long as they maintain order], in the form of Communist rule, was sacrosanct. No brick could be removed from the edifice for fear of bringing it all tumbling down.

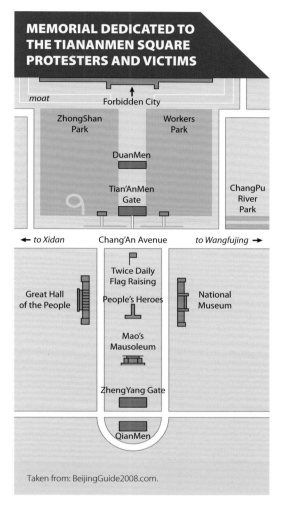

MEMORIAL DEDICATED TO THE TIANANMEN SQUARE PROTESTERS AND VICTIMS

Taken from: BeijingGuide2008.com.

As protest spread to more than 100 cities and the citizens and workers of Beijing rallied in support, the reaction was not to question where the regime might be going wrong, but for the leaders—with the exception of Zhao and his adviser, Bao Tong—to dig in their feet. When the people of Beijing peacefully stopped the tanks on their first sorties into the city, the consternation in the leadership compound was palpable. So the hardliners triumphed; martial law was declared; Zhao was ousted; and, on the night of June 3, the tanks did not allow themselves to be stopped on their way to the square.

Unleashing the Tanks

That reaction from the top and the regime's inability to handle protest peacefully made June 4, 1989, a crucial moment in China's modern history. Deng could have taken a different decision, to seek a reasonable way for-

On June 5, 1989, a single protester interrupted the progress of tanks into Beijing in defiance of the government's top-down approach to national rule. (**AP Images.**)

ward, admitting criticism and debate to try to solidify a regime which needed to grapple with the wider issues raised by the economic reform he had unleashed. It would have been difficult and messy, but it was not out of the question, and would have given him a unique place in history.

By putting the primacy of monopoly power first, the aged patriarch closed off a key avenue of potential progress for China and, once he had re-launched his drive for the market in 1992, gambled all on material progress being sufficient to give the Communist party popular legitimacy. That has made the people of China far better off, if in a highly unequal manner, and transformed the isolated Maoist state into a global player. A "China model" has emerged. People are, individually, far freer than they were under Mao, so long as they are not seen to represent any political threat to the regime. There is much lively debate in thinktanks and among intellectuals about whether to head right or left economically.

But it all remains cast in the one-party mode. The "Beijing Coma" cocoon imposed in 1989 remains in place. That provides the essential context for the burgeoning superpower, and has set China on a path by which it thinks it can defy western nostrums and pursue its own path. That is why June 4, 1989 has to be remembered, not only to honour the dead, but also to understand the rising global power.

CHAPTER 2

Controversies Surrounding the Tiananmen Square Protests

China Must Join the Wave of Reform Movements in Other Communist Countries

Wang Dan

The following selection is a March 4, 1989, article by Wang Dan, who became one of the student leaders of the protests in Tiananmen Square in the spring of 1989. Wang, a history major at Beijing University, edited a student magazine called *New May Fourth*, whose title echoed an earlier democracy movement in China, and he also convened regular meetings of other students, a so-called Democracy Forum. After the Tiananmen crackdown, Wang went into hiding but was arrested in 1990 and served three years in prison. He continued to speak out after his release and, in 1996, was sentenced to eleven more years in prison. He currently lives in the United States.

Photo on previous page: Students and other protesters opposed what they saw as corruption throughout China's ruling party, taking out their frustrations on a famous image of Chairman Mao at the Forbidden City. (**AP Images.**)

SOURCE. Wang Dan, *Voices from Tiananmen Square: Beijing Spring and the Democracy Movement*. Montreal, Quebec: Black Rose Books, 1990. Copyright © 1990 Black Rose Books Ltd. Reproduced by permission. www.blackrosebooks.net.

Wang writes of numerous reform movements in Communist states in Eastern Europe, including those of years earlier which had ended in violence, oppression, and authoritarianism. He emphasizes, however, changes taking place in Poland, Hungary, and Czechoslovakia where large demonstrations had resulted in greater political openness and, in the Polish case, the end of one-party rule. Writing on March 4, only three months before the crackdown in Tiananmen Square, Wang would have had no idea that in those three European countries, Communist regimes would end by December 1989.

More than thirty years ago, [Soviet leader Nikita] Khrushchev's secret report to the CPSU [Communist Party of the Soviet Union, in which he criticized predecessor Joseph Stalin], the Polish and Hungarian events [anticommunist demonstrations in the 1950s], and our own Hundred Flowers Movement [a brief period of political debate in 1956 and 1957], provided moments of scintillating possibility for an international communist movement hovering on the edge of irrelevance. The saddest thing was that each was followed by a long period of military-autocratic rule in those countries. Today, however, eastern Europe is again reminding us of the spirit of 1956.

In February 1989, the Hungarian Socialist Workers' Party [the ruling Communist party] recognised the 1956 events as a "genuine people's uprising." The Hungarian party congress affirmed a multiparty system and pluralism, with the formation even of a "non-party faction."

Face-to-face meetings in Poland have produced concrete results, with opposition organizations like Solidarity and the Writers' Union, having been legalised, organising massive demonstrations. On February 10th, Premier Jaruzelski declared that

> We think that the path taken by Poland, Hungary, and Czechoslovakia is the only way to save socialist countries from their internal crises.

the Polish United Workers' Party would be "giving up its monopoly of power."

In Czechoslovakia, in spite of the caution and indecisiveness of the regime, there have been frequent and decisive actions by the masses. Recently, over one thousand cultural workers petitioned Premier Strougal to demand the release of students arrested in the Prague demonstrations in January.

What is happening in eastern Europe should teach us two things. First, we see that the dictatorship of one party (or some similar system known by a different name) should be abandoned, the introduction of democratic politics being a major trend in socialist development. It is now obvious that a refusal to reform the political system is an attempt to protect vested interests, and is against the tide of change. Second, the promising developments in

A visit to China in May 1989 by Mikhail Gorbachev (left), who brought reforms to the Soviet system, gave hope to reform-minded students on Tiananmen Square. (**AP Images.**)

those countries must be attributed to the ceaseless efforts of the opposition inside both the party and the general population. Their prolonged and untiring efforts in pursuit of freedom of speech and the protection of human rights is responsible for the creation of a healthy political atmosphere. It also reaffirms that democracy is not a gift, but the product of struggle from below by the people themselves. In this struggle, the educated elite must play a leading role by acting as a vanguard.

We think that the path taken by Poland, Hungary and Czechoslovakia is the only way to save socialist countries from their internal crises. Political developments in China must learn from these countries. Let us bluntly state: Only when China follows in the footsteps of these eastern European countries, and only then, will full democracy and full development be successfully accomplished.

March 4, 1989

Democracy in China Is Rising Up from the People

Fang Lizhi

For the first 30 years of its existence, following the Communist takeover in 1949, Chinese leaders such as Mao Zedong practiced strict state control of the economy. New leaders who emerged following Mao's death in 1975, notably Deng Xiaoping, began to lift economic restrictions and allow more free enterprise. What followed were many years of economic growth and development. In the following selection reformer Fang Lizhi, a prominent figure whose work is considered a major inspiration for the 1989 protests, wonders whether this economic development will be accompanied by cultural and political reforms.

Writing at the beginning of 1989, Fang argues that 40 years of Communist rule taught the Chinese people to be dependent on their leaders, a state of affairs the government encouraged for the sake of stability and order. Recent protests, including student demonstrations, showed that some people had thrown off

SOURCE. Fang Lizhi, "China Needs Democracy," *Liberation (Paris)*, January 17, 1989, p. 5. FBIS, January 27, 1989, pp. 14–16. Reproduced by permission.

their government dependency and wanted democratic reforms. Fang suggests that the Chinese leadership's hope for a system combining a free-market economy with a one-party dictatorship will probably not succeed, and that ordinary Chinese people will continue to make demands for greater democracy. Previously a prominent academic and member of the Communist Party of China, Fang Lizhi was expelled from the Party in 1987. During the Tiananmen Square crackdown he and his wife were given asylum in the U.S. embassy in Beijing and they later moved to America. Fang is now a professor of physics at the University of Arizona and continues to speak out on behalf of human rights.

In China, 1989 is the year of the snake. Though it is not certain that this snake will present any great temptations, the following is at least to be expected: The year will prompt the Chinese to examine their past more thoroughly and to take a more penetrating look at the present. The year will mark both the seventieth anniversary of the May 1919 Movement (an intellectual and political movement of prime importance against a background of nationalism and Western cultural influence [also known as the May Fourth Movement]) and the 40th anniversary of the founding of socialist China. These two anniversaries can serve as eloquent symbols of China's hope and despair.

These forty years of socialism have left the people in a state of dependence. In the fifties, watchwords such as "only socialism can save China" or "there is no New China without the Communist Party" were as readily accepted as laws of physics. Now a glance at the "New" China suggests that the naïve sincerity of those years and the people's enthusiasm have been betrayed.

Of course, the past forty years have not been entirely devoid of change or progress. However, the comparative criterion for measuring the failure or success of a society should be this: Has the distance between China and the world's most advanced societies increased or not? In

Chinese astrophysicist Fang Lizhi became a leading dissident voice through his critique of Marxism and support for democracy in his native land. (**AP Images.**)

light of this question, not only have the forty years of Maoist China been a failure but even the past ten "years of reform" have produced nothing to justify a chorus of praise.

The failure of the past forty years cannot be attributed—at least not entirely—to China's cultural tradition.

> In China today the pursuit of modernization has replaced faith in ideology.

The facts clearly show that almost all of the other nations proceeding from bases similar to China's have already joined, or are about to join, the ranks of the developed countries.

Nor can this failure be attributed to China's overpopulation. First, we must recognize that this overpopulation is itself one of the "political successes" of the Maoist years. It was Mao's policy in the 1950s to oppose birth control and to encourage rapid population growth.

China's Chaotic Twentieth Century

For more than two thousand years, going back to the third century B.C., China was governed by imperial dynasties that claimed the mandate of heaven, or the approval of the gods for their rule. But in 1911 the last of these dynasties, the Q'ing dynasty, collapsed. What followed was a century of instability, uncertainty, and, at times, great violence.

The Q'ing dynasty collapsed in part because Chinese leaders were uncertain how to respond to the challenges of the Western world. Colonial powers like Great Britain, the United States, and even Japan interfered in Chinese affairs and squabbled over Chinese territory and natural resources. Immediately following the Q'ing collapse, so-called Westernizers tried to establish a modern economy and sys-

tem of government but were thwarted by the country's divisions. Much of the countryside, in fact, lay in the hands of semi-independent warlords with their own armies. The May Fourth Movement of 1919, led by student demonstrators wanting their leaders to assert a stronger nationalism, was a dramatic interlude in this early era.

From 1919 until 1949 China suffered from political division, invasion, and civil war. While various warlords continued to hold sway in rural areas, the "Nationalists" under General Chiang Kai-Shek (Jiang Jieshi) formed a loose national government and were officially recognized as China's leaders by the outside world. Chiang's regime, however, only truly controlled the nation's large cities, particularly coastal ones. By the 1930s, mean-

Furthermore, as everyone knows, one of the major factors retarding China's economic development has been the great succession of "class struggle" campaigns and large-scale political persecutions. Are we to believe that every overpopulated society necessarily produces such struggles and persecutions? Such a view is clearly illogical.

Development, Not Ideology

Logic leads to only one conclusion: the disappointments of the past forty years must be attributed to the social sys-

while, Mao Zedong's Communist Party of China had broken from Chiang's Nationalists and was building up a strong base of support in some rural regions. Mao preached a form of communism that emphasized agricultural peasants rather than urban industrial workers. He also promised to end corruption and the broad influence of foreign countries on China's economy.

In 1931 imperial Japan conquered Manchuria, to China's north. Then in 1937 the Japanese invaded China proper. The war continued until 1945 and Japan's final defeat at the end of World War II. During those years Japan came to control almost all of China's coastline and practiced a brutal occupation resulting in millions of deaths, mostly from hunger and disease. Meanwhile, Chiang maintained

a stronghold in the city of Chongqing while Mao, working separately, built up a huge peasant army to fight Japan.

From 1945 to 1949, Chiang's Nationalists and Mao's Communists fought a civil war, uprooting still more millions. The end of the war came in 1949, when Mao marched triumphantly into the capital city of Beijing. The Nationalists, however, escaped to the island of Taiwan and continued to claim that they represented China's true and legal government. The status of Taiwan remains, in the early twenty-first century, a source of conflict. While some Taiwanese hope to establish an independent state there, China's official stance is that Taiwan is merely a "rogue province."

tem itself. This is why in China today the pursuit of modernization has replaced faith in ideology. Socialism, in its Lenin-Stalin-Mao version, has been entirely discredited. At the same time, the May 4th Movement slogan "science and democracy" is being reintroduced and becoming a new source of hope for Chinese intellectuals.

The reforms of the past years, undertaken within the context of this ideological transition, have considerably changed China, which is no longer that of the Maoist period. We must regard these changes as positive. The emphasis now being placed on the economy in domestic policy and on ending "the exporting of the revolution" in foreign policy are two important instances of progress. Having said that, the banning of the "wall of democracy" nine years ago created the depressing feeling that when it comes to political reforms the authorities do not intend to do much.

Although the Chinese Constitution guarantees freedom of speech and other human rights, the Chinese Government has hitherto not always adhered to the UN human rights charter. In current practice, even a basic right such as the right to knowledge, which has little political impact, is frequently held in contempt. There are cases—some very recent—of natural science courses being banned for political reasons.

Chinese education, which for years suffered the ravages of Mao's anti-intellectual and anti-cultural political principles, has left China with a population in which the proportion of illiterates is the same as forty years ago. Nevertheless current education spending, as a proportion of China's GNP [gross national product], is exactly the same as under Mao: 30–50 percent lower than in countries on an economic par with China.

In recent years the authorities have stepped up their appeals for "stability" and "unity," especially since the emergence of signs of political unrest. Stability and unity seem to have been elevated to the status of supreme principles. However, when it comes to one of the prime causes of the instability in Chinese society—the state of civil war maintained with Taiwan—this supreme principle no longer applies. In its attempt to end the forty-year-old state of war, the Chinese Government has hitherto refused—at least in theory—to accept the principle of relinquishing the use of military force against Taiwan.

> " What we have now is not a democracy but a dictatorship. "

These various problems have created a constant conflict under the surface of Chinese society. The 1986 student demonstrations openly demanding freedom and democracy only brought these conflicts to the surface. In their efforts to minimize the impact of these demonstrations, the authorities were forced to resort to the following arguments: (1) Chinese culture lacks a democratic tradition and therefore cannot tolerate a democratic system. (2) Economic development does not necessarily require a democratic system. Indeed, a dictatorial system can be more efficient in this regard. What would suit China best is a dictatorial policy plus a free economy.

Democracy, Not Dictatorship

The brandishing of these arguments revives public awareness that what we have now is not a democracy but a dictatorship. If this is so, however, how can Marxism retain its place in China's orthodox ideology?

The first of these arguments could be called "the law of conservation of democracy." It implies that a society's "maximum level of democracy" can be fixed. If there is no democracy to start with there will be none subsequently either. Of course nobody has tried to prove this law because there are too many examples to the contrary. The argument cannot save the dictatorship in China but it can provide some comic relief.

The second argument does seem to be better corroborated by the facts. There really do seem to be some societies that have succeeded in combining political dictatorship with a free economy. However, there are also some examples of failure among them. It follows that the issue cannot be decided simply by listing precedents but must be treated specifically in China's own particular case. Can a free economy be compatible with the specifically Chinese form of dictatorial government? A glance at the China of 1988 proves that, broadly speaking, the answer is "no."

First, China differs from other countries in that its system of dictatorship cannot accept an entirely free economy. This is because the socialist dictatorship is entirely bound to a system of "collective ownership" (actually official ownership) and its ideology is fundamentally antithetical to the kind of rights of ownership required by a free economy. Furthermore, it has already been shown—twice, rather than once—that China's dictatorial system lacks efficiency. It is enough to consider the corruption within the Communist Party itself to realize this. The ten years of "correction of party conduct" have in fact produced only an annual increase in the numbers of "unhealthy tendencies." Our minimum conclusion could be as follows: we need the public to be able to perform a greater role and we need a more independent judiciary. In practice this means more democracy.

> Democracy is more than a slogan; it is exerting its own pressure.

Small Steps Forward

China's hope for the present lies in the fact that more and more people have abandoned blind faith in the government. They have realized that the only way to social progress depends on the public's adopting a "supervisory" role. It should have the right to openly express criticisms of the authorities. The editor of a Canton [Guang-Zhou] journal recently wrote that his journal's role is to speak not on the Communist Party's behalf but on behalf of an emergent Cantonese middle class. The old idea that "you must not oppose your superiors" is losing ground. Democratic awareness is making headway. Democracy is more than a slogan; it is exerting its own pressure. The aim of this pressure is to force the authorities, gradually and by nonviolent means, to accept changes in the direction of political democracy and a free economy.

Since the period of the May 4th Movement in 1919, China's history (including the forty years since [the Communist takeover in] 1949) has proved this idea that democracy cannot be promulgated from above but that it is necessary to fight to gain it. We must not expect this to change in the decades ahead. However, it is precisely because democracy comes from below that, despite the many frustrations and disappointments of our present situation, I am still hopeful about the future.

China's Student Demonstrators Were Inspired by "Bad Elements"

China Daily

Chinese government officials rarely discussed the Tiananmen Square protests or the crackdown against them. The following selection offers one of these rare responses: excerpts of an article published on June 23, 1989, in the *China Daily*, Beijing's English-language newspaper. *China Daily* was commonly understood to be a mouthpiece for the government, as was the Chinese-language *People's Daily*.

The authors of the article suggest that the student demonstrators in Tiananmen Square were wrong in two related ways. First, they were misled by a small group of conspirators who wanted to overthrow the Communist government. Secondly, the students did not have a true understanding of the sort of democracy that was appropriate to China. The article claims

SOURCE. "Why Good Intentions May Lead to Turmoil and Riot," *China Daily (Beijing in English)*, June 23, 1989. Reproduced by permission.

that western-style democracy could not be imported into a nation at China's level of development, nor could it coexist with China's long-standing traditions. In addition, the article's authors charge, the students showed a willingness to go outside the law to pursue their goals.

M ost of the students were unaware that from the very beginning their good intentions were shaped to the ends of a handful of conspirators whose goal is to negate the leadership of the Chinese Communist Party.

In fact, as early as the beginning of 1989, these people began planning to fan disturbances through the opportunities offered by the seventieth anniversary of the [pro-democracy] May 4th Movement and the fortieth anniversary of the founding of the People's Republic of China. They advocated the "overthrow of the socialist system," and "ending the rule of the Chinese Communist Party." They said that Marxism was totally utopian.

> The students have revealed immaturity and superficiality over the last two months.

When the April 26 editorial of the *People's Daily* pointed out that their true purpose was to create chaos, they cloaked their ulterior motives by claiming they "opposed corruption."

Whenever the students seemed to calm down, these people tried to rekindle their agitation.

Influence of Antigovernment Conspirators

They egged the students on to stage strikes, hunger strikes and stop army trucks. They were actually taking the striking students hostage to pressure the government to agree to their terms.

China's leaders saw the student protesters as naive pawns for "a handful of conspirators." (**AP Images.**)

Most of the students were unaware of the scheme. But once they were unknowingly manipulated, their aspirations and enthusiasm turned to something that stripped them of their senses and reason. As a result, they were pulled farther and farther away from their original hopes. The government tried to give them an out again and again, but in vain.

Why have the students been caught in such a dilemma? The crux of the matter is that they have cast to the wind the notion of class struggle. Even the phrase "political struggle" jars on their ears. As a result, they refused to accept the stark fact that the demonstrations were being shaped to the ends of a handful of bad elements.

This is a lesson to be learned.

Students called their demonstrations "a movement for democracy." But from the very beginning they turned to means beyond the law.

On the one hand they called for "maintaining the dignity of the Constitution." On the other hand, they turned a blind eye to constitutional articles and local regulations concerning putting up posters and holding demonstrations. On the one hand, they asked for equal dialogue with the government. On the other hand, they dictated to the government who should participate in the dialogue and what questions must be answered.

> Grafting Western-style democracy to the Chinese reality is but a fantasy.

The students have revealed immaturity and superficiality over the last two months.

To begin with, their idea about the basic approach to found democratic politics in China is only skin-deep. They don't understand that China, with its long feudal traditions, underdeveloped economy and alarmingly high illiteracy rate, has a long way to go in bringing about highly developed democracy and that, therefore, only initial steps should be taken in this regard. Grafting Western-style democracy to the Chinese reality is but a fantasy.

Students Do Not Understand Democracy

Students have had much access to Western ideas since the implementation of the open-door policy, but have failed to digest them. They hold in high esteem Western representative institutions and the practice of checks and balances in government. At the same time, corruption among party and government officials and the defects in China's political set-up caused confusion in their beliefs. Moreover, the political education of the party and [Communist] Youth League among students became lax, which failed to drive home the truth: only socialism can save China. As a result, many students turned to Western democracy.

Apart from students themselves, we should study the reality in China today to find other causes which helped give rise to the chaos.

A poor country like China, which is going all out to develop its economy, faces a major problem: premature needs for material and political luxuries.

The students' pressing aspiration for democracy is the chief expression of premature political needs. Guided in a correct direction, their enthusiasm could become a driving force for the country's construction of democratic politics. Misled or pressed over-anxiously, their enthusiasm becomes a destabilizing factor. In the absence of restraint, it could go to extremes. Under such circumstances, nothing short of a fresh start can satisfy students' cravings. When things have gone that far, students' passions can be easily used by a handful of conspirators to achieve their ends. This has been borne out by the events over the past two months.

In light of this, the party and government should open up more channels for the people, students in particular, to voice their views on politics and democracy in a positive and reasonable way guaranteed by normal procedures. This will help regulate contradictions in their psychology and reinforce their capability to withstand social changes.

China's Economic Liberalization Will Likely Lead to Political Liberalization

Chris Patten

In June 1997, Great Britain returned to China the colony of Hong Kong, which had been in British hands since 1842. The author of the following selection, Chris Patten, was the last British colonial governor of Hong Kong, a region that had emerged as an economic powerhouse in its own right and where, in the years before the handover, a local democracy movement flourished. According to agreements between Britain and China, Hong Kong was to remain for fifty years a "special administrative region" rather than be fully incorporated into the Chinese state, but democratic institutions there are few.

Patten had fought on behalf of Hong Kong's democracy

SOURCE. Chris Patten, *East and West: The Last Governor of Hong Kong on Power, Freedom, and the Future*. Basingstoke. HAMPSHIRE: MacMillan (London), 1998. Copyright © Chris Patten 1998, 1999. All rights reserved. Reproduced with permission of Palgrave Macmillan and by PFD (www.pfd.co.uk) on behalf of Chris Patten.

movement, and in this selection he indicates his suspicion that, despite events, democracy will likely take hold not only there but in China as a whole. He refuses to believe that China is somehow different from other countries in its ability to match authoritarian government with free market economics, as Chinese leaders desired. In making his argument Patten quotes the Chinese official Zhao Ziyang, who in 1994 was ousted from power for making similar arguments and for being too sympathetic to Tiananmen Square's 1989 protesters.

It is self-evidently difficult to generalize about more than a billion people and their system of government in a vast country encompassing such a variety of social and economic experience, the inheritors of an astonishing culture and civilization, the subjects of the last of our century's terrible experiments in hope through tyranny. Yet living on their doorstep for years, observing their public and private behaviour, negotiating with their leaders, listening to and reading the real and the self-styled experts on their history, politics and way of life, I became increasingly convinced (as I shall argue at greater length later) that we tend to be so obsessed with the differences between China and other places and cultures that we overlook the many similarities. I do not believe that life has written different laws for the Chinese, that the customary interactions of politics, economics and social change are somehow reordered when they apply to China. Decency is decent everywhere; honesty is true; courage is brave; wickedness is evil; the same ambitions, hopes and fears crowd around and result from similar experiences in every society. Naturally, much that happens in China is opaque to outsiders, and even to the Chinese themselves; the day-to-day political struggle takes place behind the palace walls of Peking [Beijing].

> I do not believe that life has written different laws for the Chinese.

Chris Patten, who was Britain's last colonial governor over Hong Kong, backed democracy there and in mainland China. (**AP Images.**)

So Chinese politics are difficult to fathom for the same reason that totalitarian politics are always mysterious and murky. Who really knows who is up and who is down? Who accurately predicted the surprising defenestration [rejection] of the Communist Party's intelligent number three, Qiao Shi, at the last party congress? Observing Chinese politics is a little like a non-sailor watching a yachting regatta. One is aware that there is a race in progress, but one has no inkling of whether it has just started or is about to finish, of who is in the lead and who is the back marker. There is plainly a good deal of colourful maritime activity, but heaven knows what it all means.

While that is true of the prosaic struggles of Peking politics, I doubt whether the bigger and broader political canvas is so difficult to see and to understand. You do not have to be a Marxist to believe that economic development produces social transformation and leads to political change. The failure to adjust political structures to what is happening elsewhere in society means that the governing authority becomes an increasingly brittle carapace [shell]. The leadership of government may be stable, but—as in China—there is not much evidence of stability lower down.

A Tiananmen Legacy

These points were cogently made by Zhao Ziyang, the Communist Party leader who was dragged down by his colleagues for taking too moderate a position on the Tiananmen students' demonstrations in 1989. Five years after the event, the respected *Hong Kong Economic Journal* published the authentic transcript (minus a section on democracy) of Zhao's speech defending himself before his peers for his handling of the Tiananmen crisis and of the events that preceded it. It is worth quoting extensively, because it goes right to the heart of the predicament that Chinese leaders currently refuse to confront; on the quandary that threatens to wreck the system that sustains them they are 'in denial'.

> Reform [argued Zhao] includes the interaction between reform of the economic structure and reform of the political structure. As I now see it, in addition to reform of the economic system and economic development, socialism must also demonstrate its superiority in the political system and the problem of democracy. In the course of practice, in relation to reform of the economic system, I felt more and more keenly that reform of the political system should neither outstrip it nor fall behind, but rather that the two should, on the whole,

proceed at the same pace. I used to think that—so long as we did well in reforming the economic structure, developing the economy, and people's living standards went up—then the people would be satisfied and society would be stable. But as I later discovered this is not the way things are.

After living standards and cultural levels have been raised, the people's sense of democracy and sense of political participation will grow stronger. If ideological education fails to keep up, and if the building of democracy and the legal system fails to keep up, then society will not be stable. Last December, I said at a military conference that—as is clear from the conditions in many countries—economic development often cannot automatically bring about a people's contentment, satisfaction or social stability. I feel this presents us with two problems: first, we must persist in grasping with both hands and not overlook work in the ideological–political spheres. Second, reform of the political system—the building of socialist democracy and the legal system—must catch up [with the reform of the economic system].

Zhao's argument is surprising only because it was expressed by a Chinese Communist leader. In effect, he was stating what most observers assume to be the fatal flaw in the strategy of Peking's market Leninists. Just because China is the country in question, there is no reason to suppose that it is possible to open up the economy while keeping an iron grip on politics. As Margaret Thatcher [former British prime minister] argued in a speech in Peking in November 1996, 'I do not believe that in the long term [China] will be immune from the same processes which

> "Chinese Communists embarked on capitalism because Communism had so manifestly failed."

have affected its neighbours'. Rising living standards, to borrow from Mr Zhao, will strengthen 'the people's sense of democracy'.

Democracy Must Follow Economic Development

Chinese Communists embarked on capitalism because Communism had so manifestly failed, and its failures threatened to topple the party from power. With their governmental competence questioned and their moral authority in tatters, Deng and his supporters argued through the late 1970s and the 1980s that, in order to retain its control of China, the Communist Party would have to show that it could after all make people better off. The only way it could accomplish that was by modernizing China, introducing capitalism, and throwing the county's doors and windows open to the outside world. Deng's opponents argued that, far from saving the party and preserving its control over society, economic liberalization would destroy it. China's inescapable dilemma is that both sides in this argument are right.

Improvements in the living standards of parts of China, and parts of Chinese society, have bought time. To many Chinese, as [China scholar] Perry Link has argued, 'Shut up and I'll let you get rich' seemed about as good an offer as the Chinese were likely to get from their government. They preferred the freedom to make money to the absence of any freedom whatsoever. But this does not seem a solid long-term foundation for Communist Party rule. Problems crowd in on every side. There are tensions between the 'get-rich-quick' regions, principally in the south and on the eastern seaboard, and the poorer Chinese hinterland. There are also tensions between those groups in society that have been touched by the 'feel-good' factor and those who live impoverished on the fringes of society or who find themselves trapped in jobs that cannot benefit from capitalism with Chinese characteristics. The egalitarianism of rationed joy and shared hardship has been replaced by jungle-law capitalism; the egalitarian spirit of those who get left behind will have developed a sharper edge and a sourer taste. Social instability bubbles away. Corruption is pandemic, with imperceptible distinctions between graft, fraud, organized crime and accepted business practice. Violent crime stalks town and countryside. Ask a Hong Kong businessman whether he would be happy to drive home through Guangdong [a Southern Chinese Province] at night. Despite being far and away the world's number one centre for capital punishment, China is plagued by kidnappings, drug traffic, violent robberies, the sale of people (male children, for example) and the organization of illegal immigration to Europe and the United States. In the last few years, there has been a growing number of reports of unrest in the countryside and labour disputes in the cities, on whose outskirts dwells an army of migrant labour.

After Tiananmen Square, China Embraced Economic Reforms

Joseph E. Stiglitz

China's crushing of the Tiananmen Square–based democracy movement was atypical of the experiences of most other Communist countries in 1989. In Eastern Europe, demonstrators ended Communist regimes in Poland, Hungary, Czechoslovakia, East Germany, and Romania that year, with the fall of the Berlin Wall being the great symbol of those events. And by the end of 1991 the Soviet Union, the greatest Communist power of the world since 1917, had ceased to exist meaningfully. It was in the process of breaking up into a number of new independent republics, the largest of which was Russia.

In the following selection Nobel Prize–winning economist Joseph Stiglitz examines how, despite Russia's uneasy transition to democracy, it was far outpaced in terms of economic development by the communist People's Republic of China. China, he

SOURCE. *Globalization and Its Discontents* by Joseph E. Stiglitz. Copyright © 2002 by Joseph E. Stiglitz. All rights reserved. Used by permission of W.W. Norton & Company, Inc., and by the Penguin Group UK Ltd.

argues, adopted a "gradualist" or step-by-step approach that had allowed the economy, and Chinese workers, to grow accustomed to greater economic freedom. This gradualism was most notable in the process of privatization, or turning state-run enterprises over to private operators. China's successes, meanwhile, also encouraged foreign firms to invest there, which further fed the nation's rather remarkable economic growth. But, preferring stability over all, China's officials did not allow greater political freedom to accompany this economic growth. Joseph Stiglitz served as an economic adviser to President Bill Clinton from 1993 to 1997 and won the Nobel Memorial Prize in Economic Sciences in 2001. His books include *Making Globalization Work* and *Fair Trade for All*.

Similarly China's success over the past decade stands in marked contrast to Russia's failure. While China grew at an average rate of over 10 percent in the 1990s, Russia declined at an average annual rate of 5.6 percent. By the end of the decade, real incomes (so-called purchasing power) in China were comparable to those in Russia. Whereas China's transition has entailed the largest reduction in poverty in history in such a short time span (from 358 million in 1990 to 208 million in 1997, using China's admittedly lower poverty standard of $1 a day), Russia's transition has entailed one of the largest increases in poverty in history in such a short span of time (outside of war and famine).

> " China's transition has entailed the largest reduction in poverty in history in such a short time span. "

The contrast between China's strategy and that of Russia could not be clearer, and it began from the very first moves along the path to transition. China's reforms began in agriculture, with the movement from the commune (collective) system of production in agriculture to the "individual responsibility" system—effectively, *partial* privatization. It was not complete privatization:

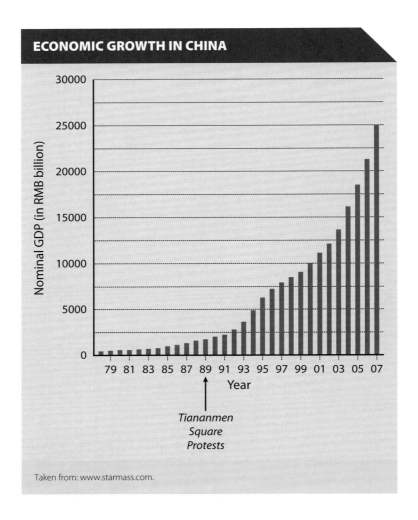

ECONOMIC GROWTH IN CHINA

Nominal GDP (in RMB billion) vs. Year

Tiananmen Square Protests

Taken from: www.starmass.com.

individuals could not buy and sell land freely; but the gains in output showed how much could be gained from even partial and limited reforms. This was an enormous achievement, involving hundreds of millions of workers, accomplished in a few years. But it was done in a way that engendered widespread support: a successful trial in one province, followed by trials in several others, equally successful. The evidence was so compelling that the central government did not have to *force* this change; it was willingly accepted. But the Chinese leadership recognized that they could not rest on their laurels, and the reforms had to extend to the entire economy.

At this juncture, they called upon several American advisers, including Kenneth Arrow and myself. Arrow had been awarded the Nobel Prize partly for his work on the foundations of a market economy; he had provided the mathematic underpinnings that explained why, *and when*, market economies work. He had also done path-breaking work on dynamics, on how economies changed. But unlike those transition gurus who marched into Russia armed with textbook economics, Arrow recognized the limitations of these textbook models. He and I each stressed the importance of competition, of creating the institutional infrastructure for a market economy. Privatization was secondary. The most challenging questions that were posed by the Chinese were questions of dynamics, and especially how to move from distorted prices to market prices. The Chinese came up with an ingenious solution: a two-tier price system in which what a firm produced under the old quotas (what it was required to produce under the old command-and-control system) is priced using old prices, but anything produced in excess of the old quota is priced using free market prices. The system allowed full incentives *at the margin*—which, as economists are well aware, is where they matter—but avoided the huge redistributions that would have occurred if the new prices were instantaneously to prevail over the entire output. It allowed the market to "grope" for the undistorted prices, a process that is not always smooth, with minimal disturbance. Most important, the Chinese gradualist approach avoided the pitfall of rampant inflation that had marked the shock therapies of Russia and the other countries under IMF tutelage, and all the dire

> Economic growth and development do not automatically confer personal freedom and civil rights.

consequences that followed, including the wiping out of savings accounts. As soon as it had accomplished its purpose, the two-tier price system was abandoned.

In the meanwhile, China unleashed a process of *creative* destruction: of eliminating the old economy by creating a new one. Millions of new enterprises were created by the townships and villages, which had been freed from the responsibility of managing agriculture and could turn their attention elsewhere. At the same time, the Chinese government invited foreign firms into the country, to participate in joint ventures. And foreign firms came in droves—China became the largest recipient of foreign direct investment among the emerging markets, and number eight in the world, below only the United States, Belgium, United Kingdom, Sweden, Germany, the Netherlands, and France. By the end of the decade, its ranking was even higher. It set out, simultaneously, to create the "institutional infrastructure"—an effective securities and exchange commission, bank regulations, and safety nets. As safety nets were put into place and new jobs were created, it began the task of restructuring the old state-owned enterprises, downsizing them as well as the government bureaucracies. In a short span of a couple of years, it privatized much of the housing stock. The tasks are far from over, the future far from clear, but this much is undisputed: the vast majority of Chinese live far better today than they did twenty years ago.

The "transition" from the authoritarianism of the ruling Communist Party in China, however, is a more difficult problem. Economic growth and development do not automatically confer personal freedom and civil rights. The interplay between politics and economics is complex. Fifty years ago, there was a widespread view

> Anyone familiar with China's history realizes that the fear of instability runs deep in this nation of over 1 billion people.

that there was a trade-off between growth and democracy. Russia, it was thought, might be able to grow faster than America, but it paid a high price. We now know that the Russians gave up their freedom but did not gain economically. There are cases of successful reforms done under dictatorship—Pinochet in Chile is one example. But the cases of dictatorships destroying their economies are even more common.

Nobel Prize–winning economist Joseph Stiglitz's work argues that China wisely sought gradual market liberalization but preserved its social status quo. (**AP Images.**)

Stability is important for growth and anyone familiar with China's history realizes that the fear of instability runs deep in this nation of over 1 billion people. Ultimately, growth and prosperity, widely shared, are necessary, if not sufficient, for long-run stability. The democracies of the West have, in turn, shown that free markets (often disciplined by governments) succeed in bringing growth and prosperity in a climate of individual freedom. As valid as these precepts are for the past, they are likely to be even more so for the New Economies of the future.

In its quest for both stability and growth, China put creating competition, new enterprises and jobs, before privatization and restructuring existing enterprises. While China recognized the importance of macrostabilization, it never confused ends with means, and it never took fighting inflation to an extreme. It recognized that if it was to maintain social stability, it had to avoid massive unemployment. Job creation had to go in tandem with restructuring. Many of its policies can be interpreted in this light. While China liberalized, it did so gradually and in ways which ensured that resources that were displaced were redeployed to more efficient uses, not left in fruitless unemployment. Monetary policy and financial institutions facilitated the creation of new enterprises and jobs. Some money did go to support inefficient state enterprises, but China thought that it was more important, not only politically but also economically, to maintain social stability, which would be undermined by high unemployment. Although China did not rapidly privatize its state enterprises, as new enterprises were created the state ones dwindled in importance, so much so that twenty years after the transition began, they accounted for only 28.2 percent of industrial production. It recognized the dangers of full capital market liberalization, while it opened itself up to foreign direct investment.

Newly Released Documents May Shed Light on the Tiananmen Square Crackdown

Daryl Lindsey

In the following selection, journalist Daryl Lindsey examines the controversies surrounding the 2001 release of a collection of documents called the "Tiananmen Papers." These were allegedly government records that had previously remained secret but were smuggled out by a man using the name Zhang Liang. Zhang was likely a Chinese official himself who had decided to make the material public.

As Lindsey writes, many people had questions over the authenticity of the Tiananmen Papers, as did the Chinese government itself. But there were also good reasons to consider them real, among them the fact that they were vouched for by three of America's top China experts. The documents portray

SOURCE. Daryl Lindsey, "A Crack in the Wall," Salon.com, February 2, 2001. This article first appeared in Salon.com, at http://www.salon .com. An online version remains in the Salon archives. Reprinted with permission.

the workings of an inner circle of high government officials, mostly older men, electing to deal decisively not only with the protests but with dissidence within the government as well. As Lindsey asserts, The Tiananmen Papers may well provide insight into both the functioning of one of the world's most closed governments and the events of spring 1989. Daryl Lindsey was an associate editor at the online news magazine *Salon.com*.

Modern revolutions aren't always clad in velvet—and they don't always win. That's what we learned when the Chinese government ordered the People's Liberation Army to use its tanks to clear the student protesters from Tiananmen Square in 1989, killing hundreds if not thousands of people. The tragedy that unfolded in Tiananmen Square remains the defining political event, with the Cultural Revolution [1966–1976], of contemporary Chinese history. But no one, aside from those involved, has ever known exactly how the Chinese leadership arrived at its fateful decision to crush the budding democracy movement. What happened inside the fortified walls of Zhongnanhai, China's leadership compound, has remained a mystery.

Until now. Maybe.

The Tiananmen Papers, published in January by Public Affairs and edited and vetted by three prominent American Sinologists [China experts], purports to be the official record of the Chinese government's struggle in deciding how to respond to the student uprising. Its appearance in Chinese this spring could have profound consequences, both social and political.

If authentic, these papers have their provenance in the highest levels of government in Zhongnanhai. Columbia University political science

'By now many of those responsible for the decision to crack down—notably Deng and others serving as "elders"—have passed away.'

professor Andrew Nathan and Princeton University professor of Chinese Perry Link edited the papers with the help of U.C. [University of California]-Berkeley journalism school dean Orville Schell, who helped vet the papers and wrote the book's afterword. The papers were compiled by the pseudonymous Zhang Liang, whose anonymity was a condition of publishing the documents.

Not surprisingly, *The Tiananmen Papers* is highly addictive reading: You want to believe every word of a publication that sheds more light on the inner workings of Chinese government than any document released in the past quarter-century. It's also one of the best-edited

Three U.S. experts on China considered the controversial *Tiananmen Papers* book a true glimpse into government decisions that led to the crackdown on dissidents. (**Alex Wong/ Newsmakers/Getty Images.**)

sets of government documents this writer has ever seen. The editors have strung together transcripts, intelligence reports, meeting minutes and editor's notes to form a riveting narrative—and one that seems highly plausible.

Questions About Sources

But this extraordinary document requires its readers to take a leap of faith. Zhang and his editors ask the reader to accept, without decisive corroborating evidence, the authenticity of documents that answer just about every question one could possibly have about the role of the Beijing government in the student crackdown.

> China has evolved much since Tiananmen . . . but it has also remained as oppressive as ever.

The paucity of biographical details about Zhang leaves a presumably unavoidable, but undeniable, cloud of uncertainty over the whole book. Zhang is either the greatest whistle-blower since Daniel Ellsberg leaked the Pentagon Papers to the *Washington Post* [in the late 1960s], or the most elaborate forger of documents since German Konrad Kujau swindled $4.8 million from *Stern* magazine for his bogus "Hitler Diaries."

All we know about Zhang, who was almost certainly an official in Zhongnanhai, is that he didn't jump ship after unfurling his load of classified documents—he stuck around for the entire process, offering corroborating evidence to give his editors enough faith in the project and his motives to attach their names to it. The presumption is that Zhang leaked the papers to light a flame under reformers who were quieted after the crackdown but are still active in the Chinese government. In his preface Zhang writes, "Reversal of the verdict on June Fourth is another historical inevitability, as well as the wish of most Chinese people. June Fourth weighs on the spirits of every Chinese patriot, and almost every Chinese knows that official reevaluation is just a matter of time. The Party's top leadership has been divided about the event ever since it occurred. By now many of those responsible for the decision to crack down—notably Deng and others serving as 'elders'—have passed away."

By publishing *The Tiananmen Papers*, Zhang apparently seeks to spark renewed debate in Beijing about the crackdown and open the door to a resumption of democratic reforms. The book's timing may even be pegged to launching a debate in the two years leading up to Chinese president Jiang Zemin's planned retirement in 2002. China has evolved much since Tiananmen—it has opened up more to the world and promotes free markets, travel and international study—but it has also remained as oppressive as ever toward the media and any groups that promote free thinking. One has only to read about the deaths of dozens of imprisoned Falun Gong [a dissident movement] followers to understand how firm and resolute the grip of the Communist Party on its people remains.

In judging Zhang's credibility, we are asked to rely on the credentials of the three men who are vouching for Zhang's book—and those credentials do carry extraordinary heft in the worlds of journalism and academia. The only physical evidence that Zhang exists was a silhouetted interview he granted CBS News' *60 Minutes* in early January and an interview he granted the *New York Times*. In that interview, Zhang told his interlocutor: "We believe that only the Communist Party has the ability in China to carry out political reform . . . In this sense we are not dissidents trying to operate from outside the system."

Critics and China experts have approached *The Tiananmen Papers* cautiously, some doubtful of its authenticity, others cautiously optimistic. No one, it seems, is taking these papers as a matter of historical fact—at least not without adding the obligatory qualifiers. The passages whose provenance raises the most questions—and they are often the most interesting—are quotes taken from private meetings at his residence between Deng, who essentially served as the shadow leader of China at the time of the Tiananmen crisis, and senior members, both active and retired, of the Communist Party. Zhang, in what appears to have been an epic breach of Zhongnanhai security, apparently had considerable access to people who had considerable access to these leaders.

Another Chinese Forgery?

The past century has seen some prominent forgeries, and both publishing houses and journalists have been duped time and again—a fact that Schell acknowledges in his afterword. And one of the more famous fakes came from China. Sir Edmund Backhouse discovered a diary in the home of Jing Shan, an assistant to the imperial family, which later became the basis for his book *China Under the Empress Dowager . . .* in the early 1900s. But years later, confidence in Backhouse's reputation has been stained by lurid tales (including insinuations that he had necrophiliac sex with the corpse of the Empress Dowager, according to *Time* magazine) and faith in his account has faded. The Oxford-trained academic didn't help his cause by failing to ever produce a copy of the diary.

The jury, meanwhile, is still out on the 1983 book by Yao Ming-Le, *The Conspiracy and Death of Lin Biao—How Mao's Chosen Successor Plotted and Failed: An Inside Account of the Most Bizarre and Mysterious Event in the History of Modern China*, which claimed that Marshal Lin Biao, a protege of Mao, was murdered for plotting to kill the Chinese leader. Last year, the daughter of the commander of the Chinese air force at the time of Biao's mysterious death, Jin Qiu, stated that after conducting her own investigation, she concluded that the book was pure innuendo. "Few students of the subject have taken this version seriously," she wrote, "chiefly because the sources to which Yao claimed to have access were never made available to others." Jin fell short of outright disproving the account, but she did successfully raise fresh doubts about its legitimacy.

The Tiananmen Papers is a different story. Strong contextual evidence suggests that it is legitimate. It has long been known, for example, that Deng Xiaoping had orchestrated the ouster of Party General Secretary Zhao Ziyang, his anointed successor, because he had been too soft on the students. Deng retired from the [ruling] Politburo in 1987, and his only official role in the government was that of chairman of the Military Affairs Commission of the party. It

> '**The national mood reflected a profound questioning of China's leaders, political system, and direction.**'

was widely reported that Deng was in fact running things even after the appointment of Zhao. But it was never before known how deep a role he played in the day-to-day decision-making about Tiananmen. The dissident writer Liu Binyan told the *New York Times* of deep splits in the Communist Party less than two weeks before the June 3 massacre; he also referred to dissent within the military, which is corroborated in *The Tiananmen Papers*.

Government Intrigue

After his meeting with Deng in May 1989, just weeks before Tiananmen, Mikhail Gorbachev [Soviet Communist leader] was bitterly criticized by Chinese officials for revealing to the foreign press that Deng was still calling the shots. But only with *The Tiananmen Papers* does the full story of Deng's involvement emerge. The power struggle between Zhao and Prime Minister Li Peng was also hinted at in media coverage of the student uprising in 1989. But *The Tiananmen Papers* are the first to document the Politburo split behind the clash.

The Tiananmen Papers takes us back to March 1989, when the Chinese government became conscious of the growing public dissent that would result in the student movement. "The national mood reflected a profound questioning of China's leaders, political system, and direction," an intelligence report cited in the book states. "But it was hard to tell whether the social contract was breaking down as a result of inflation or corruption, or a normal civil society was emerging as a result of prosperity and liberalism." The papers cover the period ending in the clearing of Tiananmen Square, with behind-the-scenes details assembled from Xinhua (China's official press vehicle), meeting transcripts, notes from telephone conversations and private conversations between the country's highest leaders.

Though Schell says there's no "smoking gun" in the documents (a fact that he says increased his belief in their authenticity) there is plenty of potentially live ammo. It has long been known that there were ideological splits at the top of the Communist Party. But what wasn't known prior to the documents' release was how deep this rift had grown during the student uprising.

The Tiananmen Papers depicts Party Secretary Zhao as a moderate figure, sympathetic to the demands of student protesters. Zhao tried to steer his fellow leaders away from declaring martial law and toward dialogue with the students. Prime Minister Li, on the other hand, comes across as an obdurate hard-liner. Deng's trusted confidante, he feared that the student uprising promoted the "bourgeois liberalism" so despised by dyed-in-the-wool Leninists and posed a serious threat to the Chinese government. A power struggle between Li and Zhao ensued. Li, who still serves on the Politburo Standing Committee but who is widely disliked both in and outside of China since the Tiananmen massacre, probably stands to lose

Deng Xiaoping

The leader of China during the Tiananmen Square demonstrations was Deng Xiaoping. Born in 1904, Deng was an earlier follower of Chinese Communist founding father Mao Zedong and played an important role in leading the armies that won China's revolution in 1949. In 1957 he rose to the level of general secretary of the Chinese Communist Party, making him one of the regime's leaders.

During the Cultural Revolution of 1966 to 1976, however, Deng fell from favor for opposing some of Mao's economic policies. He spent most of those difficult years as an ordinary worker, while his family faced attacks from the Red Guards. Indeed, one of Deng's sons, Deng Pufang, was made paralyzed while imprisoned by the Red Guards. In 1974 one of Deng's mentors, Zhou Enlai, convinced Mao to bring Deng back into the inner circles of Chinese Communist leadership. Following Mao's death in 1976, Deng was able to outmaneuver a rival, HuaGuofeng, and establish himself as the major center of power in the country's ruling politburo, or political committee. He remained in that position until his semi-retirement in 1992, although he never technically held the office of head of state.

Deng was notable among Chinese Communist leaders for his emphasis on practical solutions rather than on ideological purity. Indeed, as early as 1961 he began to utter colorful phrases hinting at his pragmatism, such as "I don't care if it's a white cat or a black cat. As long as it catches mice it is a good cat." Deng's search for practical solutions to China's lasting poverty enabled him to repudiate the Cultural Revolution and to open up China's economy slowly to free market reforms. This willingness to allow Communist ideology to be modified to include elements of free market capitalism became part of what Deng referred to as "socialism with Chinese characteristics." It has also helped the Chinese economy to be the fastest developing economy in the world since the early days of his time in power. Contemporary China, indeed, reflects another colorful phrase often attributed to Deng: "to get rich is glorious." In 1989, Deng held the office of Chairman of the Central Military Commission and was at the center of the group of "elders" which made the decision to use military force to quell the Tiananmen Square demonstrations.

Deng retired from active involvement with the government in 1992, But he still remained widely respected as the instigator of China's economic reforms and was revered as the "paramount leader." Although some of his political rivals, notably, Jiang Zemin, rose to power after his 1997 death, Deng's economic policies remain in force and his position in Chinese history is likely secure.

> It was the elders who moved unanimously to declare martial law and turn the troops on the students.

the most from the publication of *The Tiananmen Papers*, since they show that without his cheerleading for the crackdown, the events of June 3 might never have happened.

When forced to decide whether to move against the students, the Politburo Standing Committee—the highest formal decision-making body in China—split 2-2, with one member abstaining. But under a clandestine 1987 agreement, Deng, who was technically retired, and the extra-constitutional "elders" had veto power and oversight over the Politburo Standing Committee. Following the split verdict, the elders moved to purge Zhao and other leaders who sympathized with the students.

Jonathan Mirsky, who covered the Tiananmen crisis for the London *Independent*, gives an ominous account of the elders in an essay on *The Tiananmen Papers* in the Feb. 8 *New York Review of Books*. Mirsky (who largely supports the authenticity of the papers) describes them as resembling a geriatric ward of communists from China's "guerrilla period." "I recall the television pictures of the elders arriving at Deng's house in Beijing—dozing, drooling, propped up by nurses and derided as figures of fun by the demonstrators, who did not realize at the time how dangerous these men were. (Nor did we journalists)," he writes.

Deng Xiaoping's Power

It was the elders who moved unanimously to declare martial law and turn the troops on the students who had filled Tiananmen Square for weeks with their hunger strikes. And in a particularly ironic development—given that the students were pushing for democratic reforms that would include the implementation of rule of law—the elders, operating as a rubber-stamp government for

Deng, elevated the relatively obscure Shanghai Party leader Jiang Zemin to replace Zhao as party chairman. The papers reveal that the decision was taken by Deng who, it seemed, acted with ayatollah-like authority. The influence of Deng over the decision making of the elders is obvious in the following excerpts from the meeting in which they sealed Zhao's political fate:

> Deng: "After long and careful comparison, the Shanghai Party secretary, Jiang, does indeed seem a proper choice. I think he's up to the task. Comrades Chen Yun, Xiannian, and I all lean toward Comrade Jiang Zemin for general secretary. What do the rest of you think?"

> Wang Zhen: "If that's what the three of you think, then that's it. I don't know Jiang Zemin very well, but I trust Comrade Xiaoping to get it right. So let's have Jiang Zemin be general secretary."

> Deng Yingchao: "I haven't had much contact with Jiang Zemin, but from what the rest of you say about him, he seems fine. I agree that he be general secretary."

This is an explosive revelation, given that their promotion of Jiang appears to have violated the Chinese Communist Party Constitution. That document provides that the Politburo Standing Committee is responsible for selecting the president, which would make Jiang an illegitimate leader. Added to the embarrassing extent to which the documents portray Deng as the seemingly lone power behind the Communist Party of the Tiananmen era, it's not surprising that Beijing says they're bogus.

"Any attempt to play up the matter again and disrupt China by the despicable means of fabricating materials and distorting facts will be futile," Foreign Ministry spokesman Zhu Bangzao said earlier this month. But the government has yet to elaborate on which, if in fact any, of the documents have been forged or redacted in a distorting way.

The publication has other critics, however, whose motives are less dubious. Dai Qing, a Beijing writer who participated in the Tiananmen movement and was imprisoned for it, told the *Boston Globe*'s Hong Kong correspondent that she believes deep-throat Zhang "got some documents from the Chinese government, but edited some things out and created some other things with a purpose. All my friends in Beijing can't believe these papers are 100 percent true, even though famous overseas Chinese figures say they are. Some details are 100 percent wrong." When grilled by the reporter about which facts were disputed, Dai pointed to comments in the paper by Yang Shangkun (China's president at the time of the crackdown) about the son of General Xu Haidong, who apparently refused to send troops into Tiananmen Square. "Dai says that she played with Xu Haidong's children when she was a girl," the Globe reported, "and that he had no son who grew up to become a senior army officer."

"Perhaps he had a son from another marriage, but we have tried to contact such a person, and no one has heard of him," Dai told the paper.

Strange Details

Even Schell is quick to admit that there may be errors in the publication. But he stands by the document's legitimacy as a whole, saying that the revelations about how senior officials were swayed to crack down on the student movement are the closest to an accurate record we're going to get without more transparency in China's notoriously walled government.

Recently, there has been a steady drumbeat of support for the authenticity of *The Tiananmen Papers*. Singapore Senior Minister Lee Kuan Yew, asked about the papers by a journalist from Singapore's *Sunday Times* in Davos, Switzerland, last weekend, replied: "They are too detailed and too extensive. You can't have a team drawing these up." The comments of Lee, who helped create modern Singapore, have considerable credibility since he also supported the Chinese government's hard-line stance on the student movement. "There are more than 300 cities in China. When you have that kind of wildfire, you either stump it out quickly or you are burnt out yourself," Lee told the paper.

Immediately after the documents' publication, former American ambassador James Lilley, who served in Beijing during the time of the crackdown, vouched, conditionally, for their legitimacy. "I believe that the documents are authentic," he told the *New York Times.* "But I don't rule out the possibility that people might have played with the language to score certain points. In addition, the docu-

> 'We've got to be explicit and clear in opposing this turmoil.'

ments themselves contain material that is not true. For example, the reports on the C.I.A. are exaggerated and inflammatory to appeal to the paranoia of the Chinese leadership."

While it may be too soon to tell what kind of impact *The Tiananmen Papers* will have inside Zhongnanhai, some predict the reverberations will be enormous. Journalist Mirsky, who reported from Tiananmen Square in 1989, writes in his *New York Review of Books* essay of a recent interview he conducted with a former Chinese vice minister. He quotes the deposed bureaucrat as saying, "The man who tells the truth about what really happened in Beijing will rule China." Mirsky continues, "If evidence comes to light showing how China's supreme leaders planned and directed the Beijing crackdown, the results, once the ritual denials are over, would be an embarrassment within the Communist Party and possibly even a change in the official verdict that what happened throughout China in the spring of 1989 was a 'counterrevolutionary rebellion.'"

Feeding the Flames

Indeed, much of the ferocity of the students involved in the protests seemed to have been fueled by an April 26, 1989, editorial in the *People's Daily*, a Communist Party mouthpiece, published just one day after a fateful meeting of the elders at Deng's home in which he laid out the framework for the essay. "We've got to be explicit and clear in opposing this turmoil," Deng said. His comments were a de facto condemnation of the protesters, since "turmoil" was a derogatory term. The editorial forced the students into the corner. They had nothing to gain by backing off, since they would likely face reprisals from the government regardless of the outcome. The best they could do was fight to restore their honor, which they believed had been smeared by the editorial. And so started the inevitable countdown to the massacre.

A broader assessment of *The Tiananmen Papers* is expected after a Chinese-language version containing the original documents is published in April. Sinologists like Berkeley's Schell expect that the book will quickly find its way into mainland China through the *dierqu dao* or "second channel"—the black market book peddlers who sell tomes on everything from Falun Gong to voodoo spiritualism and provide an important outlet for books and literature banned by Beijing. And though Beijing has proven effective at filtering Internet content, savvy communicators will still find ways to pierce the firewall to send copies of the documents by e-mail or to serve Web pages by untraceable proxy.

With the pressure that will bring, decision makers in Zhongnanhai may be forced to revisit the events of 1989—and perhaps this time they will tell the truth. In the end, whether or not *The Tiananmen Papers* is completely accurate may be less important than whether it can force the hand of China's leaders to be more candid about the most tragically defining moment of Chinese Communism since the Cultural Revolution.

The Tiananmen Papers Are a Fabrication, Say Chinese Leaders

John Leicester

Ever since the Tiananmen Square crackdown in 1989, the Chinese government has had little to say about the events. Its position was that the harsh measures directed against protesters were necessary to maintain public order, and that foreign criticism of their decisions or tactics is neither relevant nor called for. Chinese officials had a chance to reiterate this viewpoint in 2001, when a collection of alleged government documents on the Tiananmen Square controversy was released.

As the following selection makes clear, the Chinese government, after an initial period of silence, rejected this collection of documents, titled the "Tiananmen Papers," as false. The selection's author, journalist John Leicester, writes that the government's hope of keeping the matter quiet was thwarted by such contemporary sources of information as the Internet.

SOURCE. John Leicester, "Tiananmen Papers Fake: Crackdown Protected China's Stability, Development," *CBS News/Associated Press*, January 8, 2001. Copyright © MMI The Associated Press. All rights reserved. Reprinted with permission of the Associated Press.

China's government has rejected newly published documents vividly describing how Chinese leaders split over the crushing of the 1989 Tiananmen Square protests, suggesting that the papers are fake.

> The crackdown was 'highly necessary to the stability and development of China.'

"Any attempt to play up the matter again and disrupt China by the despicable means of fabricating materi-

After publication of the "Tiananmen Papers," China's Foreign Ministry spokesman Zhu Bangzao referred in a statement to the futility of "fabricating materials" and "distorting facts." (**AP Images.**)

als and distorting facts will be futile," Foreign Ministry spokesman Zhu Bangzao said in a statement issued early Tuesday morning [January 9, 2001] via the official Xinhua News Agency.

> Despite [a media] blackout, news of the papers quietly leaked into China.

The crackdown was "highly necessary to the stability and development of China," Zhu said. He said the ruling Communist Party's "correct conclusion" about the 1989 protests would not change.

It was the first official reaction to the papers, which were purportedly smuggled out of China by a disaffected civil servant and were published over the weekend.

Beijing has long argued that the protests were an anti-government rebellion that needed to be crushed to safeguard economic growth and Communist Party rule. It has ignored calls for an investigation into the bloody June 4, 1989, crackdown, in which hundreds were killed, and sought to silence victims' relatives who have demanded redress.

Secret Government Records

Initially, the government had no comment Monday about the documents released in the United States, and China's wholly state-run media did not report them. But despite the blackout, news of the papers quietly leaked into China via the Internet, foreign radio broadcasts and word of mouth, stirring the beginnings of debate.

The documents detail conversations among late Chinese leader Deng Xiaoping, who ordered the Tiananmen crackdown, and other Communist leaders. They are said to be based on never-before-published minutes of secret high-level meetings, Chinese intelligence reports and records of Deng's private phone calls.

The civil servant who provided the documents describes himself as a Communist Party member sympathetic to reformers. They appear in *The Tiananmen Papers: The Chinese Leadership's Decision to Use Force Against Their Own People*. It was published by Public Affairs.

The papers indicate that Deng ordered the Tiananmen crackdown out of fear that demonstrators could topple the Communist regime.

They reveal deep-seated paranoia that the protests were controlled by unknown anti-communist conspirators. They also expose anxiety by the party's top leaders that the more than one million demonstrators gathered at Tiananmen Square could demand their arrest.

If genuine, scholars who translated and published the papers said, the documents offer a rare glimpse into the motivations and fears behind the communist leadership's decision to order troops into Tiananmen Square.

An Anonymous Informer

The civil servant uses the pseudonym Zhang Liang. He now resides outside of China. He said he did not use his real name because he intends one day to return to Beijing.

Andrew Nathan, a professor of political science at Columbia University who co-edited *The Tiananmen Papers* with Perry Link, a professor of Chinese language and literature at Princeton University, said he believed revealing Zhang's identity would place him at risk.

Nathan and Link, both well-known China experts, said the documents are consistent with the smattering of information already available outside China and with the testimonies of other former officials who have since fled.

The two professors also spent hours interviewing the former civil servant. They say he painstakingly transcribed original records from files in Beijing and elsewhere onto computer disks, which he brought with him out of China.

Orville Schell, dean of the journalism school at the University of California-Berkeley and author of several books on China, worked with Nathan and Link.

He said he was skeptical about the authenticity of the documents at first. But, he said, the author's extensive knowledge of inner workings of Chinese government and the clarity of his motive in releasing documents—helping reformers now jockeying for position in Beijing—helped convince him that the work was legitimate.

In an Olympic Year, Tiananmen Square Serves as a Symbol of a New China

Kevin Johnson

In August 2008, Beijing served as the site for the Summer Olympic Games. The Olympics were considered a sort of coming-out party, an acknowledgement on the part of both China and the world that the ancient nation had once again risen to the status of a great power. Certainly many ordinary Chinese people felt great pride that their nation was to host such an important and symbolic global event as the Olympics.

In the following selection, American journalist Kevin Johnson notes how, in the months prior to the Olympics, Tiananmen Square served as a showcase of China's new status as an economic superpower. Johnson found few echoes of the 1989 protests, with one young interviewee claiming that 1989 was "history" that was no longer important. Johnson did find, how-

---

SOURCE. Kevin Johnson, "Tiananmen Square no Longer About Protest," *USA Today*, August 5, 2008. Copyright © 2008, *USA Today*. Reproduced by permission.

ever, that Chinese authorities still insisted on a strong government and military presence, as well as other restrictions, in pursuit of public order.

> 'History,' the student says, . . . 'is being made now.'

Decked out in a tight, white Gucci shirt, wide-frame shades and low-slung Calvin Kleins, Zhao Lin drove 621 miles from southern China to find his own place in history.

After a quick check of his shaggy hair, Zhao found his spot before a giant floral arrangement on Tiananmen Square. He flashed a satisfied smile and the universal two-finger peace sign before asking his mother to snap a photograph.

Never mind that Zhao, 20, doesn't know or seem to care what happened here almost 20 years ago when the government crushed a student uprising, killing hundreds.

"History," the student says, referring to the fast-approaching Olympic Games, "is being made now."

Like Zhao, Tiananmen Square, communist China's most iconic landmark, is all spiffed up for the Olympics.

Mao Zedong's giant portrait still looms over the vast public square, where he appears to look approvingly toward an equally large rotating Olympic insignia, partially obscuring the former chairman's mausoleum.

Topiary gardens depicting Olympic events and symbols of peace border each side of the plaza. The collision of images is stark and decidedly softer than those beamed throughout the world in June 1989, when tanks rolled in to put down the students.

New Decorations, Many Restrictions

Now the Chinese government is welcoming the world back to the historic plaza—but strictly on its terms.

Chinese soldiers stand ramrod straight in the suffocating heat. White iron fencing rings much of the square, where crowds of tourists are funneled through magnetometers and give up their bags for hand searches.

Earlier this week, the Beijing Municipal Government issued a bulletin reminding journalists—Chinese and foreign reporters—that they indeed are not free to roam at will without government approval and escorts.

Live television broadcasts also are being restricted to blocks of time in the morning and afternoon.

"To maintain a good order of reporting activities at the square . . . journalists are advised to make telephone appointments with the Administration Committee of the Tiananmen Area," the government warned in the written statement posted on its website.

"Priority of entry would be given to journalists with appointments. Guide service would also be provided."

Olympic-themed displays were placed at Tiananmen Square as the 20th anniversary of the protests neared. (China/Photos/Getty Images.)

The 2008 Beijing Olympics

The games of the 39th Summer Olympics were held in China's capital city of Beijing from August 8 to 24, 2008. The city was selected to host the games in 2001, beating out such rivals as Paris and Toronto. China's understanding, and the understanding of many outside observers, was that the 2008 Olympics might well mark the arrival of China on the global scene as one of the world's great powers. Indeed Li Lanqing, a prominent politician, proclaimed that "the winning of the 2008 Olympic bid is an example of the international recognition of China's social stability, economic progress, and the healthy life of the Chinese people."

Beijing underwent a major facelift for the event, with the construction of 31 new venues for sports, perhaps most notably the Beijing National Stadium, or "Bird's Nest," which can hold 90,000 people. The city's airport was also expanded, as was its subway system. Tiananmen Square was the site of many events connected with the Olympics, such as parts of the relay of the Olympic torch and, right before the games began on August 8, a large concert involving international musicians.

On the whole the Beijing Olympics were deemed a success. One reason

But Tuesday, Beijing Olympic organizers were clearly emphasizing the new softer look on the plaza.

Leading a tour of the exotic temporary gardens, Lian Guo Zhao, director of the Beijing Bureau of Gardening and Greening, said the $3 million project is the largest of its kind on the plaza.

Landscapers have installed 208 species and 400,000 flowering plants in all.

In one of the gardens, there is a replica of the distinctive National Stadium, known as the "Bird's Nest," made of vines.

The areas have their own irrigation systems. And from the start of the Games through September, the grounds will be replanted two times.

Shi Zhen Min, 58, and two friends couldn't get close enough to the living exhibits.

China's leaders were happy with the games was that they went off without incidents such as large-scale protests. Indeed, the decision to allow China to host the games was not without controversy. Many pointed to China's record on human rights, a concern underscored with the appearance of civil unrest in faraway Tibet in the earlier months of 2008. Some groups hoped to call for a boycott of the event although, in the end, few proved willing to go that far. As the games grew closer, athletes and visitors voiced concerns over air pollution in Beijing, a problem potentially bad enough that Chinese authorities placed restrictions on nearby factories and even on the use of automobiles. Such restrictions were examples of what observers saw as the government's heavy-handed approach to ensuring that the games went smoothly. In others, the government flatly denied any formal applications to protest and restricted reporters' access to certain Web sites. Moreover, it was not until July 20, 18 days before the games began, that foreign news organizations were permitted to broadcast from Tiananmen Square, the site of massive demonstrations 19 years earlier.

"This is the place to be," Shi said, cutting the air with his right fist.

"We all take a lot of pride in China. My hope is that the Olympics will help the world understand this country.

"We have 5,000 years of history here."

When the subject turned to the Tiananmen conflict nearly two decades ago, some declined to speak, but others addressed it head-on.

"There are many biases," said Zhou Yeng Hun, 30, referring to the influx of foreign tourists.

"After the Olympics, it is my hope that people have a better understanding of who we are."

China Must Learn the Truth

Tiananmen Mothers

In February 2009, the Web site of an organization known as Human Rights in China published the English translation of the following selection. It is a letter written by the Tiananmen Mothers, a group made up of the relatives of victims of the 1989 crackdown after the Tiananmen Square protests. Written nearly 20 years after the events, the letter notes that, in many fundamental ways, the Chinese government has offered little in the way of justice or even answers. The letter is addressed to the current Chinese leadership and asks for a full investigation of the crackdown, proper punishment for those involved, and compensation to the victim's families.

Please Show Courage, Break the Taboo, Face "June 4" Head-On

Open Letter by the Tiananmen Mothers

SOURCE. Tiananmen Mothers, "In an Open Letter, Tiananmen Mothers Urge China's Leaders to Investigate June 4," *Human Rights in China*, February 26, 2009. Reproduced by permission.

February 26, 2009

The Honorable Deputies of the Eleventh Session of the Second Plenary of the National People's Congress [NPC] and Committee Members of the Chinese People's Political Consultative Conference [CPPCC]:

This year marks the 20th Anniversary of the "June Fourth" Massacre.

In the last century, on June 4, 1989, the Chinese authorities launched a massacre against peaceful demonstrators and civilians in the capital, seriously violating our country's constitution and breaching their duty, as leaders of a sovereign state, to protect the people. This was an unconscionable atrocity that grew from a long-standing contempt for human rights and civil rights.

Over this long stretch of time, government authorities deliberately played down "June Fourth," forbade discussion among our people of "June Fourth," and prohibited the media from touching on "June Fourth." China has become like an airtight "iron chamber," and all the demands of the people about "June Fourth," all the anguish, lament, and moaning of the victims' relatives and the wounded of "June Fourth" have been sealed off from this "iron chamber."

Today, as the deputies and committee members of these "Two Meetings" [China's leadership bodies, the NPC and CPPCC] are stately seated in this assembly hall, can you hear the cry from "June Fourth"? Can you hear the painful sighs of the families of the victims of "June Fourth"? But now, the bloodstains of that time have long been washed away and the bullet marks rubbed out, and the site of the massacre is now decorated with exotic plants and flowers and has become a scene of peace and prosperity.

> The 'June Fourth' massacre has long secured its place in history's hall of shame.

But can all this conceal the sins of that time? Can it erase the sorrow of the relatives of the victims that deepens year after year?

No! It absolutely cannot. The "June Fourth" massacre has long secured its place in history's hall of shame. It absolutely cannot be diminished as a "political disturbance" or even a "serious political disturbance." It was nothing short of an unconscionable atrocity. No amount of force can negate the bitter reality of the hundreds and thousands of lives snatched away by guns and tanks twenty years ago.

Twenty years are not a short time; they are enough for a whole new generation to emerge. This new generation never experienced the bloodshed of that time, nor has it ever felt the desolate calm that settled on a killing field. It has passed; it seems that everything has passed. . . . In these 20 years, generations of our country's leaders have succeeded the one before, from the second generation to the third, and then the fourth. You deputies and committee members of the "Two Meetings" have also changed from session to session. The passage of time and the shift of circumstances seem to have given the party and country leaders a kind of opportunity to minimize "June Fourth" and push it to a distant corner of history.

> As of now, not a single one of the 194 dead that we have examined had any history of violence.

Even so, China's Tiananmen Mothers cannot consent. On the question of defining "June Fourth," we feel that we cannot afford to be the least bit vague. Whether to adhere to the initial interpretation or to change it, we must base it on facts and let the truth do the talking. If Deng Xiaoping, then Chairman of the Central Military Commission of the Communist Party of China, was wrong in "suppressing the counterrevolutionary rebellion," then we must overturn it and correct it through established legal procedures and publicly announce it to the whole society, and should not explain it away with the vague term of "political disturbances."

> Another year has passed now, yet we have heard nothing.

The Tiananmen Mothers have always held one belief, and that is: act and speak according to the facts; accept no lies. From the start of our inquiry activities, we would repeatedly check and verify our data regarding the person of interest. As of now, not a single one of the 194 dead that we have examined had any history of violence. They are all among the innocent victims of that massacre. They gave their lives for the sake of justice and all we can do is return justice to them, to pursue the justice that comes late to them. Otherwise, we would not be able to face the spirit of the dead.

Since 1995, our group of "June Fourth" victims and loved ones return here every year to write to the "Two Meetings" with three requests for officially acknowledging "June Fourth." They are: start new investigations on the "June Fourth" incident, publicly announce death tolls, release a list of the names of the dead; clarify each case to the family members of the dead and compensate them according to law; investigate "June Fourth" cases to determine those responsible and punish them. To summarize, our three requests are: "Truth, Compensation, Responsibility."

We have always upheld the principles of peace and reason. We appeal to the two committees and government authorities to utilize the methods of democracy and open dialogue to come to a just resolution. Yet our requests have not been discussed in the "Two Meetings."

In 2006, we suggested the following in order to end the stalemate over "June Fourth" and ensure that the situation can develop along a steady path: use the principle of tackling the simpler problems first. The divisive issues that cannot be resolved or agreed upon easily can be

痛悼爱子捷连·罹难十九周年

Ding Zilin, who co-founded the group Tiananmen Mothers to represent the families of people killed in China's 1989 crackdown on pro-democracy demonstrations, stands before a shrine commemorating her son, Jiang Jielian. (**AP Images.**)

set aside temporarily. Instead, first solve the issues that involve the basic rights of the victims and their personal interests. These issues include: 1) remove all monitoring of and restrictions on the movements of "June Fourth" victims and their families; 2) allow families of the dead to openly mourn their loved ones; 3) stop intercepting and confiscating both domestic and international humanitarian aid contributions, and return all the aid money that was previously frozen; 4) relevant government departments should, in humanitarian spirit, help the victims who are facing hard times to find employment and guarantee them a basic livelihood, without any political conditions; 5) remove political biases against the disabled victims of "June Fourth" such that they are treated as all other disabled persons in regards to communal participation and treatment by society, etc.

In 2008, we again proposed to the deputies of the "Two Meetings": in the world today, dialogue has replaced confrontation. The Chinese government advocates using dialogue to resolve differences and conflicts on international issues. Thus we have an even stronger basis to ask that the government authorities resolve the internal differences and conflicts in the same way. If we are able to use dialogue to replace confrontation on the problem of "June Fourth," it would benefit the whole country and be a blessing for all our people. The more dialogue we have, the more civility and law and order, and the less ignorance and tyranny. Dialogue does not lead society towards opposition and hatred, but rather, towards tolerance and reconciliation. Using dialogue to solve the problem of "June Fourth" is an imperative path toward societal reconciliation.

Another year has passed now, yet we have heard nothing.

We note that President Hu Jintao said the following in public not long ago: "In determining every single policy, we start and end with whether the people endorse it or not, agree with it or not, are happy with it or not, and consent to it or not." We welcome these words. If this is so, then we suggest to the NPC and CPPCC: why not eliminate the taboo of "June Fourth" and conduct a broad survey of the people's attitudes towards "June Fourth" countrywide, especially in Beijing, to find out what exactly the people endorse? What they agree with? What they are happy with? Consent to? We believe this should not be difficult to do.

But the people of China know very well that the tragic case of "June Fourth" is an "ironclad case" created single-handedly by the second generation leader, Deng Xiaoping. . . . [to continue the "Whatever" policies Deng pursued] Even if "suppressing the counterrevolutionary rebellion" is relabeled as a "serious political disturbance," the judgment, in essence, still has not changed.

This then will require each deputy to demonstrate extraordinary courage and resourcefulness, political courage and wisdom, to break the taboo and face head-on the unspeakable tragedy that took place 20 years ago and resolve "June Fourth" with the truth. If this should happen, you will have brought a great blessing upon our people and your achievement will go down in history.

On the Twentieth Anniversary, Tiananmen Square Is Remembered Everywhere But China

Los Angeles Times

The *Los Angeles Times* was founded in 1881 and is the second-largest metropolitan newspaper in the United States.

In the following selection, writers for the *Los Angeles Times* relate a chronology of their experiences at Tiananmen Square on June 4, 2009—the twentieth anniversary of the military crackdown by the People's Liberation Army of China that left unknown numbers of student protesters and ordinary civilians dead or wounded. Guards and plainclothes policemen outnumber tourists and visitors on the square, and ordinary citizens prefer not to discuss what they call "6-4"—a shorthand term for June 4. While the rest of the world mourns the victims, China continues to offer no official accounting of or explanation for the events that transpired in 1989.

SOURCE. Times Staff Writers, "No Ordinary Day at Tiananmen Square," *Los Angeles Times*, June 4, 2009. Copyright © 2009 Los Angeles Times. Reproduced by permission.

> "There are commemorative ceremonies all around the world. . . . Almost everywhere . . . but here, where it happened."

4:45 A.M. The sky is still murky with night when the hard-core convene at Tiananmen Square. Only the most patriotic Chinese and the most dedicated tourists have yanked themselves out of bed to watch the Chinese flag rising over Beijing at sunrise.

As the sun peeks out over the high-rises of the nearby financial district, the guards in military regalia goose-step to the flagpole for the daily ritual in front of the iconic portrait of Mao Tse-tung. The billowing red flag climbs slowly to an accompaniment of the Chinese national anthem pumped out of loudspeakers posted around the square.

Just like every other day, people snap pictures of themselves in front of the "Gate of Heavenly Peace" (*Tiananmen*, in Chinese), where Mao proclaimed the

Twenty years after the protests, China welcomed the world back to its historic square—but strictly on its own well-controlled terms. **(AP Images.)**

founding of the nation in 1949. Just like every other day, they line up at the mausoleum where his body lies preserved under glass and pose next to the 10-story obelisk Monument to the People's Heroes.

> The authorities look not just for weapons, but also for paper and scarves that might be unfurled into a banner.

But this day is not like every other day. It is June 4 [2009], the 20th anniversary of the brutal crackdown by the Chinese army that left hundreds of pro-democracy demonstrators dead.

On this day, there are commemorative ceremonies all around the world—in Washington, London, Hong Kong, Los Angeles. Almost everywhere, it would seem, but here, where it happened.

Dissidents around China have been put under house arrest to prevent any attempt to enter the square. The foreign media have been barred for the day. The entire 10 acres are fenced off with police barricades. White tents like the ones used for the happier occasion of last summer's Olympic Games are outfitted with metal detectors. The authorities look not just for weapons, but also for papers and scarves that might be unfurled into a banner.

Some visitors are asked to show their passports; those who have Chinese "J" visas (the letter indicating the holder is a journalist) are turned away.

5:20 A.M. The crowd thins out after the flag-raising is finished. About 200 are left, mostly people from Chinese tour groups wearing matching hats. A few old men are flying kites.

It is becoming increasingly apparent that there will be more security than actual visitors at Tiananmen Square today.

10:30 A.M. Buses are lined up in neat rows at the south end of the square. They look like ordinary tour buses, but the people piling out are clearly not ordinary tourists. They're all male. They carry umbrellas to shield themselves from the sun—a habit that is common for Chinese women, unusual for men. Many wear matching outfits and carry matching umbrellas. About a dozen paunchy middle-aged men wear red polo shirts and have little black wires dangling from their ears. A group of younger men wears pink T-shirts. Another group wears purple.

Hardly anybody wears white. In past few days (before the Chinese government blocked Twitter, Hotmail and a dozen other sites), the word was spreading that people should come to the square in white, the traditional Chinese color of mourning. But nobody has dared.

2 P.M. As the temperatures rise, so do the umbrellas. Tiananmen Square looks like a vast ocean of umbrellas, bobbing around like little boats on the waves. The plain-clothes policemen wield their matching umbrellas like shields. They not only want to block the sun; they hide coyly behind their umbrellas to prevent people from taking their photographs.

There must be seven or eight security personnel for every regular visitor at the square. A construction supervisor says he was told by the police that 200,000 would be deployed for the day around Tiananmen.

"They're really afraid that the students might do something again," says the man, who of course does not give his name.

In fact, he is chattier about the unspeakable than most people at Tiananmen Square. A middle-aged woman selling umbrellas here lowers her voice to a whisper when asked about the large number of police.

"Don't you know? It's 6-4," she says, using the shorthand (like 9/11) to refer to a tragedy too enormous to elaborate. "But better not to talk about that."

Even the real tourists are on edge. A Chinese guide speaking in English to a group of mostly Korean tourists lowers his voice as well to advise his wards to behave themselves.

"We're where we are, so no shouting, no running, no fooling around. Don't act stupid."

7:15 P.M. An afternoon shower has washed away the heat. A large crowd has gathered to watch the flag-lowering ceremony at sunset. The mood is almost festive. A man has made a picnic blanket for himself with a map of Beijing. He sits and takes off his loafers. A Western tourist sits on the ground and enjoys a large green bottle of local beer.

7:35 P.M. The sun is ducking behind a line of trees northwest of the square. The guards begin to lower the flag. The crowd hushes and presses forward toward the barriers. Children are lifted onto parents' shoulders. A young hipster lightheartedly sings the opening lines of the "Internationale"— the Communist anthem.

7:45 P.M. A public address system asks people to leave the square in an orderly fashion. One plainclothes policeman says to another, "Goodbye, I'm taking a car home."

The square is closed off. The anniversary has come and gone for Tiananmen.

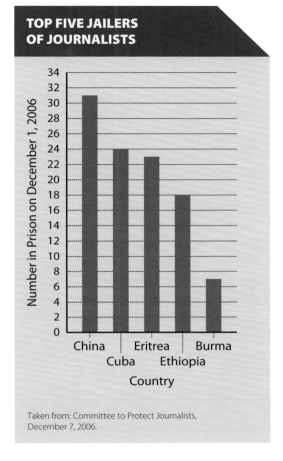

TOP FIVE JAILERS OF JOURNALISTS

Taken from: Committee to Protect Journalists, December 7, 2006.

CHAPTER 3

Personal Narratives

A Man and His Wife Make the Decision to Escape

Zhang Boli

The following selection was written by Zhang Boli, a journalism student who emerged as one of the leaders of the 1989 protests in Tiananmen Square. Following the government's crackdown, he remained a wanted fugitive until an eventual escape to Hong Kong. Zhang ultimately reached the United States and is now a pastor at a Chinese Christian church near Washington, D.C.

In the selection, Zhang describes how he and other student protesters made their way out of Tiananmen Square early in the morning of June 4. Their retreat, he claims, came in the face of great violence against the protesters. They eventually reached the campus of Beijing University, where Zhang decided that his new priority was to escape China with his wife.

Photo on previous page: A Tiananmen Square monument depicting Mao Tse-Tung became a platform for Beijing University students who sought reform in China. (**AP Images.**)

SOURCE. Zhang Boli, *Escape from China: The Long Journey from Tiananmen to Freedom.* New York: Washington Square Press, 1998. Translated by Kwee Kian Low. Copyright © 1998 by Zhang Boli. English translation copyright © 2002 by Washington Square Press. Reprinted with the permission of Atria Books, a Division of Simon & Schuster, Inc.

June 4, 1989. In the predawn darkness we were forced to evacuate Tiananmen Square. Negotiations with the army were completed. The terms we agreed upon were simple: we should leave before daybreak. A peaceful conclusion to the occupation of this largest of public gathering places in all of China seemed within reach. Helmeted soldiers allowed us to pass through the narrow corridor at the southeast side of the square, all the while pointing their bayonets, as if we were prisoners of war. Army commanders had promised to give the demonstrators an opportunity to disperse. The process, time-consuming because the crowd was huge, seemed under way.

> A great dramatic spectacle, seen on television screens around the world, had reached its climax.

"Fascist!" a female student cursed furiously. Immediately, several soldiers rushed at her and beat her down with the butts of their rifles. Her male comrades hurried to help her back into the march. And thus commenced the last phase of a major confrontation between nonviolent demonstrators led by university students and the armed forces of the People's Republic of China. On the one side, words: speeches, pamphlets, poems, petitions, the weapons of persuasion. On the other side, dictatorial power: guns, bullets, and tanks, the weapons of destruction.

For more than fifty days, student idealists, naive but brave, had done all that they could to persuade their government by peaceful means to redress their grievances. A small group at first, their numbers had grown to the hundreds and then to the thousands. Now, amplified by ordinary citizens, they had grown to the tens of thousands. At times, more than a hundred thousand. A great dramatic spectacle, seen on television screens around the world, had reached its climax.

And now an elite battalion of soldiers was moving to crush the Democracy Movement by brute force. As the day progressed, these soldiers, seemingly devoid of humanity, were to march against their own fellow citizens and employ lethal force.

As soon as we began moving away from the square, the air was filled with the roar of tanks speeding ahead. I looked back and saw the statue of the Goddess of Democracy being torn down. Rows of tents, so geometrically ordered, were being crushed by the tanks' treads, the canvas sheets sometimes flying into the air like snowflakes driven by the wind. We marched and looked back through tears of anguish. The square we had occupied for fourteen days after the government had declared martial law was now an army's playground for the enjoyment of brutal games. In addition to our fears and rage, we felt a profound sense of humiliation. All of our noble words, our passionate deeds, our bravery in the face of enormous odds were being mocked; we had entered a realm of madness and were at the mercy of men—the soldiers and their leaders—who were utterly without humanity.

Arriving at Liubu Avenue, we found that West Changan Street was still filled with the acrid nitric acid smoke of small arms and artillery fire. Here and there, military vehicles, buses, and tanks burned furiously. Destruction and horror everywhere. I turned on my pocket radio. The Central People's Radio was broadcasting an editorial of the *Liberation Army Daily News*, defining the nature of our democracy movement as "counter-revolutionary upheaval." A movement that had endured for over fifty days, designed to provide an example of direct democracy at work, was dismissed as merely a crazy grab for power. The radio announcers lied to the world. Chaos, anarchy, destruction of revolutionary ideals: these were said to be our goals. They accused the student protestors

> Students rushing up behind us said that the tanks had crushed eleven students to death.

Zhang Boli's role in the 1989 protests made him a fugitive afterward. Eventually he made his way to the United States. (Paul Richards/AFP/Getty Images.)

of conspiring to overthrow the government. Not only the government but socialism itself: all that the workers, soldiers, and peasants had sought to achieve.

West Changan Street was stained red. A man who had been beaten was covered with blood and was spitting bloody foam onto the street. Chai Ling, her face contorted with horror, cried, "He's still alive!"

I asked my schoolmates to take the man to the hospital's emergency room on a tricycle, but he died before they could get there.

Singing "The Internationale," we marched like a slow and boiling river that flowed toward Beijing University. Behind us we heard the thunder of tanks and the explosion of tear gas bombs. My tears flowed freely; I had no mask. It was so unbearable! Students rushing up behind us said that the tanks had crushed eleven students to death.

Li Lu suddenly said: "Wait a minute! We should go back! It's not right to just abandon the square!" Chai Ling and Feng Congde said nothing to show what they were feeling. Most of us opposed the idea of returning to the square. It was entirely unrealistic and we knew that. We would be met by overwhelming force and violence. The government would show no mercy. Nearly a hundred tanks and more than a hundred thousand soldiers guarded Tiananmen. If we returned it would be to die. To me it seemed that saving our lives, perhaps to fight again soon, should be the highest principle at this moment. Our responsibility was to bring as many students as possible safely back to the university.

> '_I can no longer belong to a party that has lost all rationality and humanity!_'

Mo Xuan, our picket leader, said, "You guys are the commanders. I will lead the march wherever you say!" So Chai Ling, Feng Congde, and I continued our way at the head of the throng, leading students back to the university. Li Lu and Mo Xuan turned part of the march back toward the square. Not many students followed, and those who did soon returned to follow us. We all hated to leave the square after so many days but this was what we had to do.

Arriving at a big hotel near the zoo, we saw a huge banner hanging from an upper floor. It said: "Insist on the Four Fundamental Principles. Oppose bourgeois liberalization. Take a clear-cut stand against upheaval. Firmly suppress the counter-revolutionary turmoil." We ran angrily into the hotel and tore the banners to shreds. Then we sat down to catch our breath. I had shouted so much into the bullhorn that my voice was hoarse. Now I was very tired and wanted to rest. But this was impossible.

We finally reached Beijing University at noon.

On both sides of the street from Zhongguancun to the university were crowds awaiting our return—among them teachers, students, and parents. A fifty-year-old female teacher asked me: "Where is my daughter? Did she return with you?" I stood silent with my tears flowing. Emotion was adding to the flood produced by tear gas. The entrance and the buildings around were crowded with people. Students sat down, packed like sardines with their schoolmates and teachers. I took the bullhorn from a fellow beside me and made one last speech before fleeing Beijing.

I said, "My dear school, my dear teachers and schoolfellows, we are back. We were ruthlessly driven out of Tiananmen Square by savage soldiers with tanks, rifles, and tear gas bombs. But many of our schoolmates remain forever in the square and on East and West Changan Street. When they left this world, a world they loved so much, they didn't know that those who killed them were 'the most lovely ones,' as soldiers were called by our national leaders."

I continued. "Chai Ling, Li Lu, Feng Congde, and I, as the leaders, persisted to the end in the square. We tried our best not to lose face for Beida and her students."

Weeping arose from inside and out. I spoke my last words. "Now, the fatuous old dictator has finally torn off his mask and shown his grim face. He ordered the army to shoot us! He had the tanks run over students and defenseless residents of Beijing! The soldiers didn't even stop for old people and little children. They killed indiscriminately. They arrested people to create red terror and rule by violence. And yet they label us as 'ruffians'! As 'traitors'! 'Counter-revolutionaries.' Dear schoolmates and teachers, our leaders have lost their minds. Soon they will arrest and try to kill us. They will implement a totally relentless political persecution in every part of China. Many who are loyal, high-minded citizens, including distinguished intellectuals, will be beaten, put on trial, arrested, thrown into prison, perhaps even killed. However, we are not afraid. For the truth is with us, the people are with us, the world is with us, and I believe the day will come when the light of democracy and freedom shines over all of China! On that day, if I am still alive, I shall return. I shall return here where our movement began to pay tribute to our dear school, and to my brave teachers and schoolmates. Good-bye, Beida! Good-bye!"

Suddenly a voice cried out from the crowd: "Zhang Boli! Aren't you a Communist?" It sounded strange and sarcastic.

I responded, "Yes, I am a Communist, but since the Party commanded its army to shoot the people, I have sworn to withdraw from the Party and to struggle to the end. I can no longer belong to a party that has lost all rationality and humanity!"

Applause came from everywhere like a rainstorm. I heard people shouting: Yes! Withdraw from the Party! Withdraw from this autocratic, murderous, old man's Party!

We went into the university surrounded by thousands. The picket team organized by the Beijing University Preparatory Committee immediately locked the gate, preparing for the last struggle against the troops who would soon arrive. I went to the twenty-eighth floor.

At this moment, a student of the Writers' Class came and found me; my wife, Li Yan, had arrived. How amazing! I was completely surprised. How could she have come to Beida now?

Chai Ling said: "Go and see her! There is nothing else to do but escape." I replied with a classical Chinese aphorism: "'As long as the green mountains are saved, there is always firewood.' Take care of yourselves," I said, "you and Feng Congde."

"You too," she said. "If there is really no way out, try the coast."

"I cannot leave the country right now," I said. "I have to take Li Yan out of Beijing first."

We held each other's hands tightly. Chai Ling was trembling. We knew that perhaps we would never see each other again.

A Student Mourns the Tiananmen Square Victims but Remains Optimistic

Anonymous

In the following selection, a student protester remembers his experiences the night of June 3–4, 1989. That night, the student protests in Tiananmen Square came to an end with, as this student remembers, violence and bloodshed. The author of this eyewitness account remained anonymous so that he could not be targeted by Chinese officials, either for his participation in the protests or for speaking out afterward. He made his statements on June 4.

The student notes that, by late afternoon on June 3, student protesters realized that the government was about to take action against them, although it was by no means clear what that action might be. He remembers also that the students were

---

SOURCE. *Voices from Tiananmen Square: Beijing Spring and the Democracy Movement.* Montreal, Quebec: Black Rose Books, 1990. Copyright © 1990 Black Rose Books Ltd. Reproduced by permission. www.blackrosebooks.net.

decisive in having done the right things, although they were very nervous as well. The evacuation of the square began at 4:00 A.M. on June 4 as did, the student reports, violence against the students. Even though he left the square, he returned to see many dead and injured students, including some of his schoolmates.

I am a twenty-year-old student of Qinghua University. Last night I sat on the steps of the Monument to the People's Heroes [in Tiananmen Square], and witnessed the whole incident in which the army shot the students and the citizens.

Some of my schoolmates were shot dead. My clothes are still stained with their blood. As an eyewitness and survivor, I disclose what I saw during the massacre to all kind and peace-loving people.

In truth, we knew that the army would actively suppress us yesterday afternoon. A person called on us at 4:00 P.M. and told us that the army would use violence to clear everybody from the Square. After we were told this we discussed the matter urgently. We decided to adopt some measures to alleviate the conflict and to avoid great bloodshed.

> We were encouraged by a noble feeling that it was worthwhile to sacrifice ourselves for democracy and development in China.

At that time we had 23 guns and some bombs, which were obtained from the army during the conflict which occurred in the previous two days. The Autonomous Students Union of Beijing Universities (ASUBU) decided to give these back to the army to demonstrate our principle of "Promoting Democracy by Non-Violence." Last night we contacted the army under the Tiananmen Wall. An officer replied that they could not accept the weapons by order of senior-ranking officials. Following that, the students destroyed these weapons at 1:00 A.M. because the situation had turned critical, and these weapons might have been used as "evidence" of killing soldiers.

Tense Negotiations

ASUBU announced that the situation was getting worse. Since bloodshed could not be avoided, some students and citizens had to leave the Square. But there were forty to fifty thousand students and a hundred thousand citizens who decided to remain behind. I also remained.

The atmosphere was very tense. The students had never experienced anything like this. They were certainly frightened, but they were fully prepared psychologically, their minds were firm, and many students thought that the soldiers would not open fire. Anyway, we were encouraged by a noble feeling that it was worthwhile to sacrifice ourselves for democracy and development in China.

After midnight, when two armoured vehicles sped through the two sides of the Square, the situation became much more serious. The loudspeakers of the army repeated an announcement that we should leave. Many soldiers in battledress invaded the Square from the surrounding streets. In the darkness, machine guns were set at the top of the Historical Museum.

All the students were forced to retreat to the area around the Monument of the People's Heroes. I remember that one-third were girls, and the rest were boys. Students from Beijing's higher educational institutions made up 30%, the rest being students from other provinces or cities.

At 4:00 A.M. the lights in the Square were extinguished. Again we were told to evacuate the Square. My heart pounded, as if it were saying: the time has come, the time has come. At that moment, some people who joined the hunger strike, including Hou Dejian (a popular songwriter), negotiated with the army. They agreed

> I couldn't believe that the students were so brave. They rushed at the vehicles. Many were killed.

that the students could leave peacefully. However, when the students prepared to leave, the lights in the Square were turned on. Some red flares exploded in the sky at 4:40 A.M. I saw that many soldiers had occupied the area in front of the Square. A large group of them ran out from the eastern door of the Hall of the People. They wore uniforms, helmets and gas-masks, and carried guns. (At 6:00 P.M. on June 3rd, we had spoken with a regiment of soldiers outside the western door of the Hall. They had said that they were only a supporting regiment, and that later there would be an army from Sichuan which would deal with the students directly. Their spokesman guaranteed that they would not shoot. Therefore, the soldiers who now came out were in all probability from Sichuan).

The Violence Begins

When these soldiers appeared they assembled in a row, ten or so machine guns, in front of the Monument. The gunmen all crouched down on the ground with their guns pointing towards the Monument. When this was done, many soldiers and armed police, carrying flashlights, rubber clubs, whips and various weapons, rushed towards the passive students. They attacked violently, forcing the students to separate into two groups, and move upwards on the Monument. I saw forty to fifty students with blood on their faces. Just at that moment, many armoured vehicles and soldiers moved forward. These vehicles totally surrounded us, only leaving a gap in the direction of the Museum.

The soldiers and armed police who followed us up to the third level of the Monument destroyed all our broadcasting equipment, printing machines and everything else. Then they hit the students and forced them to go down. We did not move, but held our hands tightly, singing "The Internationale" [a Communist anthem] and shouting, "The People's Army would not hurt people." But the attack was so violent that we were eventually forced to move down.

When we reached the ground the machine guns opened fire. Some soldiers knelt down to shoot, and their bullets just flew over our heads. But others aimed low, and their bullets hit the chests and heads of the students. We had to go up the Monument again, then the machine guns stopped firing. But the soldiers there forced us down again. Once again we were shot by the machine guns.

Meanwhile, some workers and citizens dashed towards the soldiers brandishing bottles and clubs. Then the ASUBU ordered us to retreat outward from the Square. The time was a little before 5:00 A.M. Students then began to rush towards the spaces between the armoured vehicles. These were closed by other vehicles. Moreover, more than thirty armoured vehicles were driven at people. Some students were run over. The flagpoles were destroyed in this way. Thus the whole Square was in a state of chaos. I couldn't believe that the students were so brave. They rushed at the vehicles. Many were killed. Others stepped over the dead bodies and ran forward again. At last there was a gap, and something like three thousand students dashed out, reaching the Historical Museum. Only a little more than one thousand of these were to survive.

There were many citizens there. Together we tried to go north, but there was gunfire. So we went towards the Qianmen Gate at the south end of the Square. I was running and crying. There was a mass of students running out under gunfire. Many people fell down. When we reached Qianmen, soldiers rushed towards us from the Jewellery Market (Zhubao Shi). They carried large clubs and hit us fiercely. Many people fought with the soldiers, which allowed us to run towards the Beijing Railway Station. The soldiers chased us from behind.

It was 5:00 A.M. and the gunfire started to diminish. Later I met one schoolmate at the International Red Cross. He told me that only those who ran from the Square could have survived. The machine guns had been firing non-stop for about twenty minutes.

A Friend Injured

The most unforgettable person was one of my friends from the college. He was bleeding but kept on running with us. Later he collapsed and fell on my shoulders. He said: "Please help me!" At that time I was holding two female school friends and could not help him. He fell down on the ground. People stepped on him. . . . He was certainly dead. Look! There is still blood on my back! There was blood covering half of his body!

> Corpses were lying all over the Square.

I shall never forget how, when some students were shot, others recovered their dead bodies, or saved those who were injured. Some girls took off their clothes to bandage the injuries of others, until they had no more to take off.

At 6.30 A.M. two school friends and I went back to the Square. There were many people there, and we followed them to the Memorial Hall, at which point we could not go any further. There were several rows of vehicles and walls of soldiers. So I climbed up a tree at the roadside, noticing that some soldiers used large plastic bags to carry away the dead bodies of students and citizens. These were piled up and covered by a large piece of canvas.

I met a school friend who had left the Square later than me. He said that many people were dead. Soldiers even refused to let the ambulances of the International

Red Cross help the injured people. We went to the First Aid Centre at the Gate of Peace (Hepingmen). We saw that many injured people were carried there by cycle rickshaws. A doctor told me that an ambulance was shot at by the soldiers and was on fire. Some injured students said that many injured students were still lying in the Square.

Around 7:20 A.M. I went back to the Square and talked with several people. They said that corpses were lying all over the Square. Soldiers covered them with cloth so that nobody could look at them. Vehicles were carrying the bodies to some unknown place. About 7:30 A.M. the soldiers suddenly shot tear gas towards the people around the Square, then they rushed towards them. I ran to the Beijing Railway Station again. I saw several students there, all crying.

ASUBU had given us Beijing students an assignment: to lead students from other places to the Railway Station. I took them to the Waiting Room, but the staff told us that all trains were cancelled. We were leaving when some citizens approached us, saying that they would take the students to their homes for protection. Many people were in deep sorrow and cried. The citizens of Beijing are really good.

How many people were killed? I'm not certain. But I believe that some day the killers must pay!

Pessimistic? No, I'm not, because I have seen China's future in the goodness of the people! Some of my schoolmates are dead, and many are injured. But I'm alive, I know how to live, and I'll remember all of the dead students. I surely know that all righteous people in the world will understand and will support us!

June 4, 1989

An American Journalist Escapes the Tiananmen Square Crackdown

Harrison E. Salisbury

Many of the specific events of the Tiananmen Square crackdown remain mysterious. While initial accounts suggested that hundreds of students were killed by the Chinese People's Liberation Army in the square itself, recent research suggests that those initial reports were exaggerations. While some students died and a number were injured in the evacuation of Tiananmen Square in the early morning hours of June 4, 1989, most of the victims of the crackdown died in the streets surrounding the square over the next days. Journalist and China expert Harrison Salisbury gives a sense of those Beijing streets in the following selection.

Salisbury kept a diary of his experiences in Beijing and elsewhere in China while he was there at work on a television documentary. His diary covered the period from June 1 to June 13, 1989. In the following portion of the diary, he records his

---

SOURCE. Harrison Salisbury, *Tiananmen Diary: Thirteen Days in June.* New York: Little, Brown and Company, 1989. Copyright © 1989 by Harrison E. Salisbury. All rights reserved. Reproduced by permission.

observations when he and his colleagues were given clearance to leave the city via the Beijing airport on June 5. They traveled through some of the city's narrow streets, where Salisbury noted that in some respects the townspeople carried on their everyday lives. But the grim presence of the army, and of clashes in the streets, could still be seen. Interestingly, even though he was on the scene, Salisbury had no clear idea of the events of the crackdown and received some reports of them by phone from his wife, Charlotte, in Connecticut, who was watching American television news. Harrison Salisbury's books on *China include China: 100 Years of Revolution* and *The New Emperors: China in the Era of Mao and Deng.*

I was just waiting for the 7:00 A.M. BBC to come on when Takeda telephoned. CCTV was picking us up in an hour to go to the airport to catch the plane for Wuhan. I hadn't bothered to pack up my junk. I had figured we were stuck in Beijing for another day. I listened to BBC. The death toll now believed to be in the thousands. I was astonished. All the calculations I had heard had put it in the hundreds, maybe three hundred altogether. They said that more clashes were going on in the city. I could hardly believe that, but there had to be some explanation, I suppose, for the absolutely overwhelming amount of firing that I have recorded and the astonishing concentration of armored troops. Someone is firing at someone or something. Why and what are beyond me. But I am damn certain a lot of it is deliberate terror shooting. They want to paralyze the people with fear, and I suspect they are beginning to achieve their purpose.

> They want to paralyze the people with fear, and I suspect they are beginning to achieve their purpose.

I called Charlotte. This direct-dial telephone system is a miracle. I just punch the call into the touch-tone phone and in ten seconds it is ringing in Taconic, Connecticut.

I understand the Chinese Defense Ministry insisted on installing this system, one of the most advanced in the world. They bought it from the French telephone company. It is in operation all over China. I can bring any city I want on-line just as fast as Taconic. No interference in this system so far. Maybe it can't be cut off without cutting off military use of it.

Charlotte was watching CBS. The two CBS newsmen had been released nineteen hours after they were picked up in Tiananmen Square. Also she had seen incredible footage of the PLA mowing down the kids on Tiananmen. There were rumors, she said, that internal air service had been suspended [this was widespread but not true], that there were battles in Shanghai, and that the railroad had been blocked for several hours but was now clear. I told her the good news—that we were getting out of Beijing—and that I would phone her from Wuhan.

> The soldiers were shooting at anyone moving on the street.

Then I packed up my gear and before 8:00 A.M. I was downstairs, where the minibus was waiting at the front door of the hotel. We all packed in—the five-man crew, Takeda, and myself, and we gave a lift to two Taiwan ladies who had been stranded at the hotel. They had come on a tour but had decided to break off and go back to Taipei. We were minus Miss He who was trapped in her building. A nest of tanks occupied the courtyard, and it was too dangerous to go out. The soldiers were shooting at anyone moving on the street. Besides, she had no way of getting to the airport and our driver didn't believe he could get through the streets to pick her up.

The driver was a very experienced man who knew Beijing almost by heart. No traffic was moving on Changan Avenue, and there were military patrols and blockades on all the principal streets and intersections. Many of the bus barricades were still in place. He would have to pick his way carefully through the network of old *hutangs*, the classic narrow Beijing alleyways, and try to find a path around the many obstacles. It might take several hours and he was not sure he would be able to do it. But it was worth a try. Our plane wasn't due to leave until 1:30 P.M., and knowing the dilatory nature of CAAC, China's civil air service, no one thought it would be taking off before midafternoon.

There were a handful of bikers on Changan as we started out, but we avoided them by doubling back to the narrow entrance on Wangfujing, which flanks the east end of the hotel. This is Beijing's main shopping street, always crowded with people, and I was surprised to see that as soon as we slipped into it and got away from the intersection with Changan, which was still a tangled mass of burned metal and rubble—the carcasses of a number of buses and cars—Wangfu-jing Street was lively and filled with people on foot and on bicycles. But no vehicles. Beijingers had already managed to find ways through their city's old streets and were out about their business despite the blockades, the tanks, and the intermittent continued gunfire.

> We passed the body of a man or woman lying at the side of the street. There were seven or eight people clustered around it.

We had made our way down Wangfujing only a couple of blocks when the intersection was blocked by a barricade we could not get around. The driver ducked into a hutang and proceeded slowly. The alley was just a bit wider than the body of the car. The scene seemed entirely normal. Women had already hung out their washing on strings from the windows. Men in trousers and white cotton undershirts were eating a breakfast of rice, picking it out of their bowls with chopsticks. Many little shops with open fronts, shoe repair men, sidewalk quick-food shops with charcoal braziers blazing, little vegetable stalls (not much but cabbage on the wooden counter), a barber serving perhaps his first customer of the day, putting lather on his face.

We had come within a hundred feet of a main street when the driver saw that the street was blocked, so he dived back into a branching hutang and began on a very circuitous course that I thought must be taking us farther and farther from any street toward the northwest—and probably that was true, although I quickly lost all sense of direction. One hutang looked like another, lined with narrow one-story buildings, most of them old courtyard houses in typical Beijing gray bricks and gray fluted roofs of slate. At one point I noticed seven- and eight-year-old schoolchildren, all dressed up in bright frocks with white aprons and red ribbons in their hair.

A bit farther we came to their school. It had a narrow play yard along the hutang, and there on the cinder surface were some ten- or twelve-year-olds playing basketball. We eased past the schoolyard and took a couple more turns, and then we were stuck. The hutang was just wide enough for us to pass and there was a dull green car, a Japanese make of some kind, blocking the hutang, not dead center but close enough so that we could not move. The car's driver was sitting in it. It was stuck. Either the motor had died or it was out of gas. I didn't think even our skillful driver could back the minibus all the way back to the last turnoff. But fortunately we had a bus full of young and energetic photographers. They leapt out, got a couple of Chinese to help them, and shoved and pushed and half lifted the car over to the side so that our bus could scrape by.

All through the hutangs we encountered little groups of people with serious faces, obviously discussing the events of the last forty-eight hours. I watched one woman with a wet cloth, carefully cleaning a wash line before hanging out her wash. Just beyond was a vegetable stand that seemed to have a normal stock of leeks and onions and celery and cabbage. Some food supplies obviously were getting into the city despite the blockage of so many roads. The hutangs were much more crowded than usual because everyone was avoiding the main streets. We came up on a string of little children with red kerchiefs heading for their schoolyard. Women were sweeping the dust from their courtyards.

At one point we came out on the little lane of the antiquities stores and restored old restaurants just north of the Qian Men Hotel, where Charlotte and I stayed on our first visit to Beijing, in 1972. The antiquities shops, as might be expected, were closed, their shutters down. I have no notion how we arrived there. We plunged into another hutang, and I was quickly totally lost once again.

Just after that we passed the body of a man or woman lying at the side of the street. There were seven or eight people clustered around it. I suppose he or she must have been shot only shortly before we passed by. No way of telling why or how or who. No troops visible in the vicinity. Most likely just the victim of one of the ten thousand random shots fired off by the "martial law troops," as the radio has begun to call them.

We kept coming up behind barricades of buses, some of them still burning. These must have been set afire within the last hour or so. Some were smoldering as though they had been burning all night. There was lots of smoke. Many barricades were all burned out. Fired yesterday, no doubt. Occasionally we were able to edge around a barricade. Usually, however, we had to back off, take a turn into another hutang, and try again. Slow progress.

I keep wondering why the PLA has made no effort to clean up these barricades. Why haven't they put wreckers on the streets to haul them away? None of the picture-postcard TV shots of the PLA show them with dirty hands. It is as if they *want* the barricades in place, as if they *want* to tie up the city. They don't seem to have any patrols out to check people on the streets, to control traffic through or around the barricades. All of that was being done by the students before the crackdown. Or by the traffic police, who even stayed at their posts all around Tiananmen until the end. Just weird.

Once we got out of the central part of the city, thanks to the beehive of the hutangs, we were more or less in the clear. We got onto the main highways leading toward the airport. For the most part, they were clear of obstruction except, mysteriously, an elephant chain of brand-new, unburned, unharmed buses. They were strung across an intersection in such a way as to block, or half block, traffic in four directions. It seemed to me that this elephant chain had to have been put in place sometime in early morning or it would have shown signs of damage. It just sat there, and the crush of bicycles, pedestrians, and our minibus managed to edge around it and go on.

But who was in charge? No one that I could see. If the army had taken over the city it had done it in the most slovenly manner imaginable—as though it had some hidden agenda all its own.

A Chinese Soldier Remembers Tiananmen Square

Christopher Bodeen

In the following selection, journalist Christopher Bodeen interviews Zhang Shijun, who as a twenty-one-year-old soldier served with a Chinese army unit, which took part in the clearing of Tiananmen Square the night of June 3–4, 1989. Zhang remains one of the few soldiers to take part in the incident who has spoken out publicly. Bodeen's interview took place nearly 20 years after the Tiananmen Square crackdown.

Zhang remembers that after the soldiers received their orders to clear the square, they moved toward it while facing objects thrown at them, and even gunfire, from buildings surrounding the square. He says little about the evacuation of the student protesters, suggesting that any stories of atrocities are "still too sensitive to tell." And although he served as a medic, and therefore was not armed, his involvement in the crackdown inspired him to leave the army early. In 1992 he was arrested

SOURCE. Christopher Bodeen, "Soldier's Story: A New Look at Tiananmen Crackdown," Associated Press, March 18, 2009. Reprinted with permission of the Associated Press.

and sentenced to prison, a sentence Zhang felt could be traced to his leaving the army in the aftermath of Tiananmen Square. Bodeen reports that Zhang continues to feel pressure from Chinese authorities.

Even 20 years later, the shooting, chaos and death of the final assault on Tiananmen Square remain vivid in the mind of former soldier Zhang Shijun. Today, he has become one of the few to publicly voice regret.

> 'I feel like my spirit is stuck there on the night of June 3.'

In bearing witness about his role in the military crackdown on the 1989 student demonstrations in Beijing, Zhang says he hopes to add momentum to calls for an investigation and reassessment of the protest movement—and to further its ultimate goal of a democratic China.

"I feel like my spirit is stuck there on the night of June 3," Zhang, 40, said in an interview at his home in the dusty northern city of Tengzhou, referring to the date in 1989 on which the final assault began.

Zhang's tortured memories have gained a global audience among the Chinese dissident community in the weeks since he posted an open letter to president and Communist Party leader Hu Jintao online. In it, he relates some of what he saw when posted on the night of June 3–4, along with an account of the persecution he underwent after asking for an early discharge, and his belief that China must eventually clear its collective conscience of the tragic events.

"The responsibility can't just be laid on the military," Zhang said. "It's really the responsibility of all Chinese."

Zhang was just 18 when he joined the elite 54th Group Army's 162nd Motorized Infantry Division based in the central city of Anyang. Less than three years later, with

student-led protests gathering pace, Zhang's units were ordered to Beijing on April 20, 1989. There, they camped on the capital's southwestern edge while citizens erected barricades to block their progress toward Tiananmen, the vast square in the heart of the city where the students had established their headquarters.

On June 3, their orders came: Drive through to the square and get it cleared.

Almost 20 years after he helped end the Tiananmen protests as a member of China's armed forces, Zhang Shijun publicly expressed regret over his actions. (**AP Images.**)

Attacks on Soldiers Outside the Square

Heading east toward the square, Zhang and his comrades abandoned their vehicles as bricks and rocks flew at their heads and bullets were fired at them by unknown shooters from upper stories of apartment buildings. Members of his unit fired over the heads of civilians as a warning, said Zhang, who added that he himself was serving as a medic and unarmed in the final assault.

Zhang said he knew of no deaths caused by the troops of the 54th army—a claim impossible to disprove as long as official files on the events remain closed. Most of the post-crackdown reports pinned the hundreds, possibly thousands of deaths among civilians and students on two other units, the 27th and 38th group armies based outside Beijing.

By daylight the next morning, Zhang said his unit established a cordon along the square's southern edge between a KFC restaurant and the mausoleum of communist China's founder, Mao Zedong.

Zhang said other details were still too sensitive to tell, suggesting atrocities such as the shooting in the back of unarmed students and civilians. While other eyewitnesses have made similar allegations, they remain impossible to independently confirm.

After their withdrawal, Zhang said he asked for and eventually obtained an early discharge, never having expected to be sent to fight ordinary citizens. After returning to Tengzhou he began a discussion group promoting market economics and politics, but was arrested on March 14, 1992, and sentenced to three years in a labor camp for political crimes. Then, as now, he regarded the charges as trumped-up retribution for his leaving his unit early.

After his release, Zhang said he traveled to find work, returning to Tengzhou in 2004 to deal in arts and antiques and help raise his 13-year-old daughter. In a dingy study adorned with his calligraphy and curio collection, he spends hours at the keyboard of his battered computer keeping in touch with other dissidents and surfing the Internet politics discussion boards.

Zhang, who retains the close-clipped haircut and restrained demeanor of a military man, said he came forward partly to seek redress for his jail camp term, but that revisiting the Tiananmen events remained his main focus.

> 'Democracy just seems further and further away.'

Few Soldiers Have Spoken Out

"Back then, we felt that it would all be addressed in the near future. But . . . democracy just seems further and further away," Zhang said between puffs on an endless string of "General" brand Chinese cigarettes.

Zhang said he hoped his example would inspire more ex-soldiers to come forward and form a network, but appeared reluctant to cast himself as an organizer, perhaps wary of the party's tendency to single out perceived opposition ringleaders for harsher punishment.

Already, his activities have aroused official attention. Visitors have been followed by police and Zhang said authorities who summoned him Wednesday, a day after the AP interviewed him, ordered him to shun the foreign media.

Retired professor Ding Zilin, an advocate for Tiananmen victims whose teenage son was killed in the crackdown, said Zhang is one of only a few soldiers to speak up about the 1989 events. Many who took part in the crackdown continue to hide their involvement, refusing to wear the commemorative watch issued to all martial law troops, she said.

"Twenty years have passed, but if the soldiers still had conscience, there may be others who stand up," Ding said.

Nicholas Bequelin, Asia researcher for New York–based Human Rights Watch, said testimony from those who took part in the crackdown was invaluable to forming a full view of the events.

That Zhang was willing to come forward, Bequelin said, simply reinforced the conviction among many that "in the long run, a reassessment of those events is inevitable."

CHRONOLOGY

1911	China's last imperial dynasty, the Q'ing, is overthrown.
1919	In the May Fourth Movement, students demand reforms.
1949	Mao Zedong's Communist Party of China succeeds in taking the country, inaugurating the People's Republic of China.
1956–1957	In the brief Hundred Flowers Movement, communist leaders are open to criticism and new ideas.
1958–1961	The Great Leap Forward, an attempt at rapid industrialization, results in millions of deaths from starvation and disease.
1966–1976	China's Great Proletarian Cultural Revolution retards economic development and intensifies internal strife.
1978	Deng Xiaoping emerges as China's supreme politician and begins to open up China's economy.
1986–1987	A wave of student protests demands political change and an end to corruption.
1987	Hu Yaobang, general secretary of the Chinese Communist Party, is forced to resign for being too open to reforms.
April 15, 1989	Hu Yaobang dies. His death becomes the occasion for new student protests.

The Tiananmen Square Protests of 1989

April 17, 1989	Students from Beijing University begin protests in Tiananmen Square. They are soon joined by students from other universities.
April 19, 1989	A first clash between students and government police occurs outside Xinhuamen, a building that serves as the entrance to a government compound for high-ranking officials.
April 21, 1989	Renewed protests bring more than 100,000 students to Tiananmen Square.
April 26, 1989	The Chinese government prepares to bring military units into Beijing to keep order in the capital.
April 29, 1989	Students form the Autonomous Student's Union of Beijing Universities (ASUBU) to guide the protests.
May 4, 1989	Some 200,000 students march toward Tiananmen Square. Beijing residents cheer them on.
May 13, 1989	Upset that the government will not speak with ASUBU and that their protests are not receiving enough media attention, some student leaders begin a hunger strike.
May 15, 1989	More than 100 hunger-strikers are hospitalized. The number of protesters and supporters in Tiananmen Square reaches 800,000.
May 17, 1989	Leading politician Zhao Ziyang pledges no reprisals against student protesters.
May 19, 1989	Following a meeting with Zhao Ziyang and General Secretary Li Peng, students call off their hunger strike, only to resume it the next day.
	Zhao Ziyang resigns. Li Peng and Deng Xiaoping grow

more impatient with what they deem "public disorder" and declare martial law on May 20.

May 21, 1989   As many as one million people gather in Tiananmen Square. The government cuts satellite access for foreign media broadcasters.

May 26, 1989   Student leaders make tentative plans to retreat from Tiananmen Square on May 30. The retreat is later delayed to June 20, the date of an important government meeting.

May 30, 1989   The statue "Goddess of Democracy" is wheeled into Tiananmen Square.

June 2, 1989   Two hundred thousand Chinese soldiers are in and around Beijing; their movements are impeded by both civilian and student protesters.

June 3, 1989   At 6:00 P.M., the Chinese government announces that a violent suppression of the protests is imminent.

At 10:00 P.M., Chinese soldiers open fire on people to prevent them from entering Tiananmen Square.

June 4, 1989   At 5:00 A.M., student protesters leave Tiananmen Square as the violence continues on the streets outside.

June 5, 1989   An unknown "tank man" is photographed trying to stop the movement of a line of tanks by standing in front of them.

June 9, 1989   Deng Xiaoping makes a public statement praising the army for ending the protests while Chinese television releases a list of twenty-one wanted protest leaders.

FOR FURTHER READING

Books

Stephen Angle and Marina Svensson, eds., *The Chinese Human Rights Reader: Documents and Commentary*. Armonk, NY: Sharpe, 2002.

Timothy Brook, *Quelling the People: Military Suppression of the Beijing Democracy Movement*. New York: Oxford University Press, 1992.

Lee Feigon, *China Rising: The Meaning of Tiananmen*. Chicago: Dee, 1997.

Rob Gifford, *China Road: Journey Into the Future of a Rising Power*. New York: Random House, 2008.

George Hicks, ed., *The Broken Mirror: China After Tiananmen*. London: Longman Current Affairs, 1990.

Nicholas D. Kristof and Sheryl Wudunn, *China Wakes: The Struggle for the Soul of a Rising Power*. New York: Times Books, 1994.

Joshua Kurlantzik, *Charm Offensive: How China's Soft Power Is Transforming the World*. New Haven, CT: Yale University Press, 2007.

Peter Li, Marjorie H. Li, and Steven Marks, eds., *Culture and Politics in China: An Anatomy of Tiananmen Square*. New York: Transaction, 2007.

James Miles, *Legacy of Tiananmen: China in Disarray*. Ann Arbor: University of Michigan Press, 1998.

Mok Chiu Yu and J. Frank Harrison, eds., *Voices from Tiananmen Square: Beijing Spring and the Democracy Movement*. Montreal: Black Rose Books, 1990.

Michel Oksenberg, Lawrence R. Sullivan, and Marc Lambert, eds., *Beijing Spring, 1989: Confrontation and Conflict, the Basic Documents*. Armonk, NY: Sharpe, 1990.

Minxin Pei, *China's Trapped Transition: The Limits of Developmental Autocracy.* Cambridge, MA: Harvard University Press, 2006.

Tony Saich, ed., *The Chinese People's Movement: Perspectives on Spring 1989.* Armonk, NY: Sharpe, 1990.

Harrison E. Salisbury, *Tiananmen Diary: Thirteen Days in June.* Boston: Little, Brown, 1989.

Orville Schell, *Mandate of Heaven.* New York: Simon and Schuster, 1994.

Susan L. Shirk, *China: Fragile Superpower.* New York: Oxford University Press, 2007.

Shen Tong with Marianne Yen, *Almost a Revolution.* Boston: Houghton Mifflin, 1990.

Suisheng Zhao, ed., *China and Democracy: The Prospect for a Democratic China.* New York: Routledge, 2000.

Yi Mu and Mark V. Thompson, *Crisis at Tiananmen: Reform and Reality in Modern China.* San Francisco: China Books and Periodicals, 1989.

Periodicals

Audra Ang, "Tiananmen 20 Years Later: A Survivor's Story." Associated Press/ABC News, April 11, 2009.

Melissa August et al., "Ten Years After Tiananmen," *Time,* May 31, 1999.

Todd Carrel, "Beijing," *National Geographic,* June 12, 1999.

"China Braces for Tiananmen Square Massacre Anniversary," *Australia News,* April 13, 2009.

Gregory Clark, "The Tiananmen Square Massacre Myth," *Japan Times,* September 15, 2004.

"Events at Tiananmen Square All But Erased from Chinese History," *Sault St. Marie Press,* May 2, 2009.

Pico Iyer, "The Unknown Rebel," *Time,* April 13, 1998.

Kari Jensen, "Hong Kong Students Vote to Condemn Tiananmen Square Violence," *Voice of America,* April 17, 2009.

Robert A. Manning, "China Closet: Facing the Legacy of Tiananmen," *New Republic*, July 20, 1998.

Andrew J. Nathan, "The Tiananmen Papers," *Foreign Affairs*, January/February 2001.

Michael Wines, "China Sees a Calendar of Trouble," *New York Times*, March 10, 2009.

Web Sites

China News Digest/June 4th (www.cnd.org/June4th). Part of a larger site on China maintained in Malaysia, this Web page offers links to documents, photographs, and resources on the Tiananmen Square incident.

China News (www.china.org.cn). This general Web site featuring news from China is continually updated.

Human Rights in China (www.hrichina.org/public). News and resources on the topic of human rights in modern China are provided on this Web site. It includes information on the continuing legacies of Tiananmen Square.

Tiananmen Square: The Gate of Heavenly Peace (www .tsquare.tv). Based on a television documentary on the Tiananmen Square protests, this site contains a general history, links, and video clips.

INDEX

YA 951.058 T43H
The Tiananmen Square protests of

FEB 1 8 2011